# PRUNING

P R A C T I C A L  G A R D E N I N G

# PRUNING

## DAVID SQUIRE

### CHANCELLOR
### PRESS

First published in Great Britain in 1995 by

CHANCELLOR PRESS

an imprint of Reed Consumer Books Limited

Michelin House, 81 Fulham Road, London SW3 6RB

and Auckland, Melbourne, Singapore and Toronto

ISBN 1-85152-842-3

A CIP catalogue record for this book
is available from the British Library

*Designed and produced by*

THE BRIDGEWATER BOOK COMPANY

*Art Director and Designer* Terry Jeavons

*Managing Editor* Anna Clarkson

*Series Editor* Penny David

*Illustrator* Vana Haggerty

*Studio photography* Guy Ryecart *assisted by Jim Clowes*

*Location photography* Steve Wooster *assisted by Carolyn Clegg*

*Typesetting and page make up* Mark Woodhams

*Produced by* Mandarin Offset

*Printed and bound in Hong Kong*

ACKNOWLEDGEMENTS

*The author would like to thank Anna Clarkson, Managing Editor,
for her dedication to the production of this book.*

*The Bridgewater Book Company would like to thank the following for their cooperation:*
*Kennedys Garden Centre, Hailsham (John Phillips); Stone Cross Nursery, Pevensey (Garth and Julie Winwood, Alick Janaway);*
*Tendring Fruit Farm, Hailsham; Hugh and Judy Johnson (Saling Hall); The Savill Garden; The Royal Botanic Gardens, Kew; The Royal Horticultural*
*Society's Garden, Wisley; Mr & Mrs Peter Aldrington (Turn End); Christopher Lloyd (Great Dixter); Mr & Mrs Huntington (The Old Rectory);*
*Mr & Mrs Potts (Chiffchaffs); Langley & Boxwood Nursery, Hampshire (for supplying topiary).*

# CONTENTS

# INTRODUCTION

Gardeners have seldom been content to leave the growth of plants solely to the fancies and whims of Mother Nature. Rather, they are shapers of their environment, experimenting with the removal of parts of plants to encourage the development of larger and better fruits and flowers, more colourful leaves and stems. Few gardening techniques have been cloaked in as much mystique as pruning, yet basically it is a simple and logical process. In temperate countries its timing is strongly influenced by the onset and retreat of winter weather that would damage young shoots. Tropical and subtropical regions also have their own growth-limiting influences, particularly droughts, both seasonal and prolonged.

In this practical step-by-step book, we deal only with pruning plants in temperate regions. Included are several pruning techniques such as bark-ringing and root-pruning which have become less widely practised due to the introduction of less vigorous and more predictable rootstocks. Nevertheless, these techniques are described as many older gardens have large, unfruitful trees that pre-date these developments.

### PRUNING TOOLS

Pruning tools should be functional as well as pleasant and easy to use. Always handle a tool before buying it, ensuring it fits your hand and feels comfortable, and always buy good-quality tools as invariably they last longer than cheap, inferior ones.

Pruning tools must be kept sharp if they are to function easily and successfully. Wash and wipe them after use and, if they are not to be used for a few weeks, lightly coat metal parts with a thin coat of oil.

Electrically powered tools are especially dangerous if not used responsibly: always install a circuit-breaking device to ensure the power is cut off should cables be severed or a fault occur with the tool. At the end of each season, have the equipment serviced by a competent electrician and replace all cables that are worn. Carefully inspect all plugs and sockets for safety.

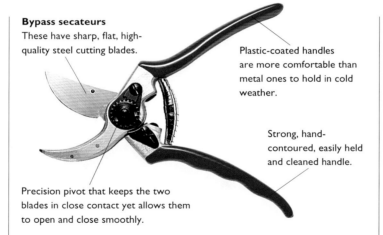

**Bypass secateurs**
These have sharp, flat, high-quality steel cutting blades.

Plastic-coated handles are more comfortable than metal ones to hold in cold weather.

Strong, hand-contoured, easily held and cleaned handle.

Precision pivot that keeps the two blades in close contact yet allows them to open and close smoothly.

**Secateurs** are available in two basic forms. The bypass model (also known as cross-over or parrot-type) has a scissor-like action and cuts when one blade passes the other (*above*). The other is an anvil type, with a sharp blade that cuts when in contact with a firm, flat, metal surface known as an anvil (*right*). Both types come in several sizes. Most secateurs are sold to suit right-handed people, but left-handed models are available.

**Anvil secateurs**

Strong, sharp, metal blade.

Anvil, against which the cutting blade closes.

WILKINSON SWORD

**Branch or tree-loppers** (*right*) are ideal for cutting shoots high on fruit trees. They cut shoots up to 25mm (1in) thick and from branches 3m (10ft) high. They are ideal for pruning large and vigorous fruit trees that have been neglected or those grafted on to too vigorous rootstocks. Do not use loppers to cut exceptionally thick or tough shoots as this will blunt the blades. After thick branches have been removed, cover any cut surfaces with a liberal coating fungicidal wound-paint to prevent any disease or infection from entering the tree. Use an old brush for this.

**Cross-over loppers**

The leverage created by long arms enables thick shoots to be easily and cleanly cut.

**Loppers** have long handles and enable thick shoots to be removed without having to use a saw. There are two types of cutting action – cross-over (*above*) and anvil (*below*). Most loppers have handles 38–45cm (15–18in) long and cut wood up to 36mm (1¹/2in) thick. Heavy-duty loppers, with handles 75cm (2¹/2ft) long, cut wood 5cm (2in) thick. Some anvil-types have a compound cutting action that enables thick branches to be cut with greater ease. Although loppers are quick and easy to use, they are soon strained if used continuously to cut excessively thick and tough shoots.

**Anvil loppers**

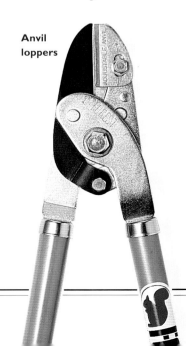

**Folding saw**

**Folding saws** are ideal for carrying in a pocket and are usually 18cm (7in) when folded, extending to 40cm (16in) long in use. Other models have 23cm (9in) long blades and extend to 55cm (22in) when unfolded. The teeth cut on both the push and pull strokes. Most folding saws cut wood 36mm (1¹/2in) thick. Replacement blades are available for most models.

**Most straight-bladed**, fixed-handled saws (*above*) cut branches 13cm (5in) thick, although high-specification ones sever branches 18cm (7in) thick. Blade lengths range from 25–30cm (10–12in) long. Replacement blades are available.

Plastic and wooden handles are available: ensure they can be easily and strongly gripped.

**Saws with curved blades** sometimes known as Grecian saws, (*above*) cut on the pull stroke. Because the blade is tapered and pointed, the saw is usable in narrow spaces.

**Bow saws** (*above*) are usually 60cm (2ft) to 90cm (3ft) long, some only 30cm (1ft). The blade is kept under tension by a lever.

**Knife**

**Knives** were once used by professional gardeners to prune shrubs and fruit trees, but unless the blade is exceptionally sharp – and combined with years of experience – both plants and hands become damaged. Pruning knives are now mainly reserved for paring cut surfaces smooth before an application of a fungicidal wound-paint. However, they are essential when bark-ringing trunks or notching and nicking buds. Knives are available in many sizes, with blades that fold into the handle. It is false economy to buy a cheap knife as the blade will need repeated sharpening and may not be strongly secured in the handle.

High-quality steel that retains a sharp cutting edge.

**Hand shears** (*above*) are ideal for trimming hedges and beds of heathers. Most models will cut stems up to the thickness of a pencil. Some have a notch near the base of each blade to enable thicker shoots to be severed. Rubber-clad handles absorb the wrist-juddering action of repeated opening and closing.

**Powered hedge clippers** (*right*) are essential where there is extensive hedging. Petrol-powered generators that power electrical hedge clippers are ideal in areas far away from power supplies. Also, cordless types cut about 83sq m (100sq yds) of hedging between recharges from a mains electricity supply. However, most types are powered by mains electricity. Cutting blades range in length from 33–75cm (13–30in) and while a few have cutting knives on one side only, others have knives on both and are therefore usable by either left- or right-handed gardeners.

# PLANTS THAT NEED PRUNING

Botanical purists might argue that even grass needs pruning to keep it at a uniform height and to encourage the development, in certain species, of shoots from the base. But it is woody plants that are the prime candidates for pruning and these come in the form of ornamental shrubs and trees (including conifers), fruit trees, bushes and canes, climbers, hedges and topiary. Roses, which enjoy something of a cult status, are deciduous flowering shrubs which need regular pruning to keep them healthy and capable of creating a radiant display each year. Pruning roses is more complex than pruning most other shrubs because there are so many different types. Their pruning is also influenced by the type of soil, whether the plant is newly planted or established, and whether it is being grown for exhibition or just for display in gardens. Throughout this book these and other variations are illustrated and explained.

### FLOWERING SHRUBS

Shrubs are among the most popular garden plants. When correctly pruned, they will produce colourful flowers each year that will last for several weeks. Some create their display in spring or summer, others in winter when there is a lack of colour. A few shrubs, such as the common dogwood (*Cornus alba*), are specifically grown for their colourful stems which brighten gardens during winter and early spring.

Other shrubs are grown for their colourful leaves: these include variegated and evergreen hollies, as well as deciduous species, such as *Philadelphus coronarius* 'Aureus', which develops fresh foliage each spring.

Many deciduous shrubs are popular for their rich leaf colours in autumn that daily grow brighter and more attractive until the leaves fall in late autumn or early winter. Berries are an important feature of some shrubs and trees, and help to brighten gardens from autumn through to late winter.

ABOVE  *Ceanothus arboreus* 'Trewithen Blue'

ABOVE  Flowering cherry tree

In temperate countries, where each year the temperature falls during autumn or early winter and plants are exposed to frosts, deciduous flowering shrubs can be divided into three groups. First are the winter-flowering types, which require little pruning and are pruned immediately their flowers fade. These include the Chinese witch hazel (*Hamamelis mollis*) and Cornelian Cherry (*Cornus mas*) with golden flowers.

The second group includes shrubs that flower at any time from spring to mid-summer. These are pruned as soon as their flowers fade, so that young growth encouraged by pruning has time to ripen and harden before the onset of winter. The third group includes shrubs that flower in late summer. For shrubs in this category pruning is delayed until spring of the following year, when they will be free from the risk of frost damage.

### TREES

Trees require less regular pruning than shrubs, although during their formative years it is essential that crossing branches are removed. Most deciduous trees are pruned in winter when dormant. Flowering cherries and other members of the prunus family, however, must be pruned in spring or early summer, when their sap is rising, to prevent the entry of diseases such as bacterial canker.

LEFT Regular clipping and pruning has ensured that this yew hedge (*Taxus baccata*) remains attractive.

RIGHT Roses need to be pruned in different ways, according to whether they are bush types, standards, hedges, climbers or ramblers. The climber *Rosa longicuspis,* with its large clusters of milky-white flowers, needs little pruning. It is shown here scrambling over the top of a wall and mixing with a variegated climber and herbaceous perennials.

## HEDGES

Hedges are an important part of gardens. Dense evergreen or coniferous hedges are especially valuable at the perimeter to make windbreaks or assure privacy. They need pruning to create attractive shapes. Small flowering shrubs used to separate one part of the garden from another are pruned to promote regular flowering. Pruning deciduous hedges helps to produce a mass of shoots from their base: hedges with thin bases are always an eyesore. In areas where there is a risk of high snowfall, the top of the hedge should be sloped so that snow quickly and easily falls off the top.

## GARDEN TOPIARY

The art of topiary was known to the Romans during the first century AD. In the following centuries its popularity waned, although during the Middle Ages plants were trained, clipped and tied to flexible stems. Nowadays, most garden topiary is formed from the common yew (*Taxus baccata*), edging box (*Buxus sempervirens* 'Suffruticosa') and shrubby honeysuckle (*Lonicera nitida*).

BELOW Apple blossom is a welcome sight in spring, but bushes and trees soon deteriorate if not pruned.

BELOW Cones, balls, pyramids and small animals can be formed from topiary.

## FRUIT TREES, BUSHES AND CANES

Fruit trees, bushes and cane fruits need regular pruning to encourage the yearly production of good-sized, healthy fruits. Pruning also helps to ensure trees do not become congested with shoots and age prematurely. Apples and pears grow in a variety of forms, including bushes, trees, pyramids, cordons and espaliers. The nature of bush-grown soft fruits varies widely: blackcurrants develop fruits on shoots produced during the previous year, while both red and white currants, together with gooseberries, have a more permanent framework. Cane fruits such as raspberries develop fresh canes each year. Canes that have produced fruits should be removed immediately the crop is picked.

RIGHT Yearly pruning is essential to keep vines healthy.

## GRAPEVINES

Grapevines are among the oldest cultivated plants. Pruning the woody structure is essential for the development of grapes as well as the training of the vine. Another part of pruning is thinning the fruits, to ensure the berries that remain reach a good size. There are several ways to prune grapes, but they all encourage the development of young shoots each year.

# ORNAMENTAL SHRUBS AND TREES

These woody plants create the framework of a garden, around which herbaceous perennials, annuals, biennials and rock-garden plants can be featured. They are the most permanent features of a garden and therefore need careful training and pruning, especially during their early years. The pruning they require varies enormously. Conifers, once established, need little attention, broad-leaved trees slightly more, while shrubs should be checked every year, if only to make sure their centres are not becoming congested with crossing stems and excessive growth. Also, a check can be made for the presence of diseases.

Before pruning any shrub or tree it is essential to know its name: the nature and flowering times of shrubs can vary widely, even within a genus and between species. The butterfly bush (*Buddleia davidii*), for example, flowers from mid- to late summer while *B. alternifolia* creates its display during early summer. It is important to ensure plants are correctly labelled or recorded in a notebook.

**SELECTING A PLANT**

Pruning is not, essentially, a way to keep a shrub, tree or conifer small. Bonsai, a specialized method of pruning that restricts growth, can be considered, but this is only suitable for small plants in shallow pots. Therefore, never buy a plant that will eventually become too large for your garden. There is always the temptation to buy the rapid-growing × *Cupressocyparis leylandii* to form a windbreak or large hedge. In most gardens this is a mistake for in fifteen years or less it can grow 15m (50ft) high.

Many trees are selected for their attractive outlines, perhaps spreading or weeping. If an excessively large variety is selected, subsequent pruning to prevent it invading neighbouring gardens may completely spoil its normally attractive appearance.

Ornamental shrubs and trees create varied shapes and colours and range from low-growing ericas (left) to flowering trees and shrubs (above), many with coloured leaves or stems. Some need only the flowers to be lightly clipped off, while with others whole stems and shoots are removed.

**REGULAR PRUNING**

Where shrubs have not been regularly pruned, they age prematurely and do not create a good display. Some may grow too large, obscuring other plants, blocking out light and draining the soil of moisture and nutrients, to the detriment of nearby plants.

If you inherit a garden full of large or neglected plants, do not rip them out straight away before considering if they can be cut back to encourage the development of new growth from their base. Some shrubs can be rejuvenated by spreading the pruning over two or three years. Additionally, feeding shrubs that have been severely pruned encourages the development of fresh shoots. Those that are a jungle of gnarled branches or thin, bare stems should be replaced with young specimens, but first improve the soil.

# PRUNING DECIDUOUS SHRUBS

Deciduous shrubs shed their leaves in autumn and develop fresh ones in spring. This enables them to survive winter in a dormant state without suffering appreciable damage, while retaining the ability to continue growth with a fresh set of leaves in spring. During severe winters, the tips of immature shoots may be damaged, but usually survival is assured unless the shrub is exceptionally tender. Not all deciduous shrubs need annual pruning, but those that do can be divided into three types according to their flowering time: 'winter', 'spring to mid-summer' and 'late summer'. The general principles of pruning these shrubs are described here, but there are many specific variations and these are detailed on pages 18 to 33. Variations include leaving on the old flower heads of *Hydrangea macrophylla* (which bears flowers during mid-summer and into autumn) until spring of the following year, when the old shoots are removed to leave young ones that will bear flowers later in the year. Leaving the old flower heads in position during winter creates protection for the shoots, as well as providing areas on which frost can create attractive patterns.

## CLIMATE VARIATIONS

To suit the climate in temperate regions, flowering deciduous shrubs are arranged in three groups. These groupings are based on the expectation that from late spring or early summer the weather will be free from frost. In reality, however, there are considerable differences in the severity of weather and the date of the last frost in spring or early summer. The local climate must therefore be taken into consideration; freezing temperatures might damage freshly developed young shoots in early summer.

In areas that rarely experience frost, pruning can be performed safely in late winter. If in any doubt about the severity and timing of frosts in your area you could consult the meteorological office. Alternatively, local horticultural clubs or gardening associations often have a very good idea of the micro-climates in particular areas.

## HEALTHY MEASURES

Whatever pruning group a shrub is in, always clear away and burn pruned wood in case the shrub is infected with diseases or harbours pests. This ensures the infection or pests will not spread to other plants.

Old, neglected deciduous shrubs sometimes become covered in algae. Renovation pruning will remove much of this, but any that is left can be removed by spraying with a winter-wash (the type used for apple and pear trees). Use this only when the shrub is dormant and free from leaves and ensure that late winter- and spring-flowering bulbs planted under and around deciduous shrubs have not appeared above the soil's surface. Take care when treading on soil, as the shoots of bulbs may be just below the surface and can be easily damaged. Shoots from early-developing herbaceous plants will also be damaged if the soil's surface is walked on.

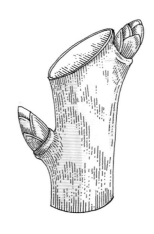

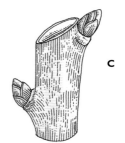

**A**

**B**

**C**

The position of a cut in relation to a bud is important and influences subsequent growth. The above illustration shows the correct position of a cut: slightly sloping, with the upper point just above a bud. If the cut slopes downwards and towards the bud (A), there is a danger that it might be damaged. If the cut is too high (B), the stub will die back and allow diseases to enter. Cuts that are positioned extremely close to the bud (C) may leave it unsupported and damaged.

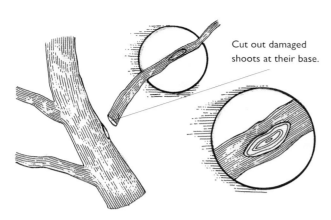

Cut out damaged
shoots at their base.

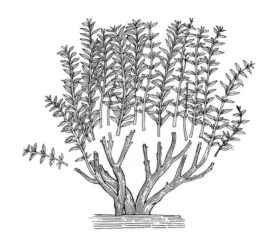

LEFT Prune the
butterfly bush (*Buddleia
davidii*) in early spring,
cutting out flowered
shoots to within a few
buds of the old wood.
Fresh shoots soon
appear in late spring
and early summer.

**Winter-flowering deciduous shrubs** need little pruning other than shaping when young and the removal of branches that cross the plant's centre, creating congestion and reducing the maturing and ripening influence of the sun. Always cut out pest- and disease-damaged shoots; if left, they encourage the decay to infect and damage other parts.

Prune winter-flowering deciduous shrubs as soon as their display is over. This gives shrubs the maximum amount of time in which to produce new shoots and for them to ripen before the onset of cold weather in the following autumn or early winter. It is easier to control the size of winter-flowering shrubs than any other type.

**Late-summer-flowering deciduous shrubs** are pruned during late spring of the following year. If pruned immediately after their flowers fade, the young shoots that subsequently develop would be damaged by frosts during winter. By leaving pruning until the following year, the fresh young shoots will not be exposed to frost.

First, cut out dead and diseased shoots, then those that cross the centre of the shrub. At the same time, cut out thin and weak shoots. Next cut to just above a bud all those shoots that produced flowers during the previous year. Pruning varies slightly according to the individual shrubs, for details see pages 18 to 33.

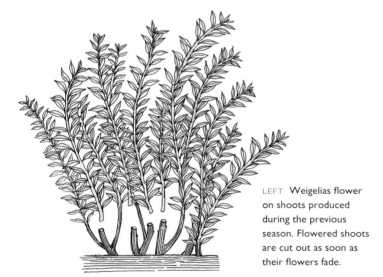

LEFT Weigelias flower
on shoots produced
during the previous
season. Flowered shoots
are cut out as soon as
their flowers fade.

**Early-flowering deciduous shrubs**, flowering between late spring and mid-summer, should be pruned as soon as their flowers fade.

First, cut out thin and weak shoots, and those that cross a shrub's centre. Then, cut out to within a couple of buds of their base all shoots that have borne

flowers. The removal of flowered shoots leaves young ones that will bear flowers during the following year. If shrubs have been neglected for several seasons, many can be rejuvenated by cutting back the complete shrub. However, this usually means foregoing flowers for one season.

## PRUNING HYDRANGEAS

Mop-head hydrangeas (*Hydrangea macrophylla*) are superb garden shrubs, which flower during mid-summer and continuing into autumn. Leave the flower stems and old flower heads in place until late winter or early spring. Then, cut out all shoots that produced flowers during the previous year. This radically thins out the shrub, allows light and air to enter and encourages the development of fresh shoots which will bear flowers later in the year.

# PRUNING EVERGREEN SHRUBS

Evergreen shrubs are clothed in leaves throughout the year, with old leaves continually falling off and new ones being formed. Once established, these shrubs need no more pruning than cutting out weak, diseased and straggly shoots in spring. Never prune evergreen shrubs in winter, as any young shoots that subsequently develop could be blackened and damaged. This could mean that pruning has to be performed again in spring, to cut out these newly developed and blackened shoots. In exceptionally cold areas, it is better to defer pruning until early summer, when there is no risk of frost.

If an evergreen shrub is grown for its spring or early-summer flowers, such as Darwin's berberis (*Berberis darwinii*), which blooms during late spring and early summer, delay pruning until after the display has faded.

Evergreen shrubs are frequently in demand by flower arrangers, especially during winter when there is a shortage of other foliage plants to choose from. When cutting attractive evergreen foliage from a garden shrub, always take stems from the back of the plant and select shoots from several positions. Use secateurs to sever them slightly above a leaf-joint and take care not to spoil the shrub's shape.

### RENOVATING EVERGREENS

The farther back into old wood that large, neglected evergreens are cut, the less likely it is that they will develop fresh shoots from their bases and become fully clothed with leaves again. Rather than cutting the entire shrub hard back in one season, it is better to spread the pruning over two seasons. During the first spring, severely cut back half of the shoots; the following spring, prune the remainder. If, after the first pruning, the shrub fails to develop sufficient shoots, cut it back less severely in the second spring.

Evergreen shrubs that respond to being cut hard back include rhododendrons, common laurel (*Prunus laurocerasus*), Portugal laurel (*P. lusitanica*), common box (*Buxus sempervirens*) and the floriferous daisy bush (*Olearia × haastii*).

### TRANSPLANTING EVERGREENS

Occasionally it is necessary to move a large, evergreen shrub from one part of a garden to another, perhaps if the area is being renovated and there are some choice but neglected specimens in it. Just digging up the shrub and moving it makes it difficult for the roots to absorb sufficient moisture to keep the leaves fresh while it is re-establishing itself. In areas where winters are mild, transplanting large evergreens is possible in autumn, when the soil is warm, but in cold areas late spring is better. Before digging up the shrub, shorten long stems and branches by a half to two-thirds. After replanting, syringe the foliage and erect a screen to protect the shrub from strong sunshine and cold winds. In spring, water the soil, and in early summer give it a feed.

RIGHT During exceptionally cold winters, evergreen shrubs often have their leaves singed and blackened by frost. The edges darken, becoming crisp and brittle. In spring, use sharp secateurs to cut out the damaged leaves, together with part of the stem. Cut close to a leaf-joint, taking care not leave short stubs, as eventually they decay and encourage the presence of diseases.

ABOVE Never use hand shears to prune large-leaved evergreens; sharp secateurs are much better.

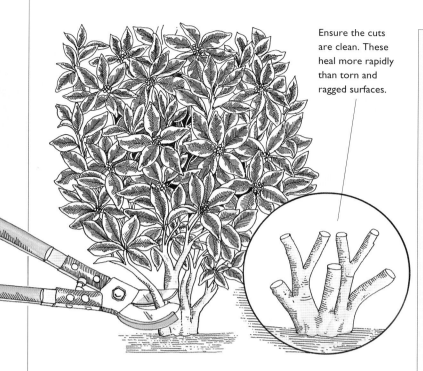

Ensure the cuts are clean. These heal more rapidly than torn and ragged surfaces.

## PRUNING LAVENDER

Lavender flowers from mid- to late summer and is pruned by lightly trimming over the plants in late summer, using a pair of sharp hand shears. Do not cut into young shoots; just trim off the old flowers. If a plant is straggly, cut the stems hard back in late spring. This encourages the development of young shoots from the plant's base. Lavender hedges are clipped to shape in spring.

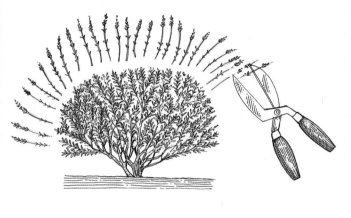

### REJUVENATING SHRUBS

Large, overgrown evergreen shrubs such as the spotted laurel or gold-dust tree (*Aucuba japonica* 'Variegata') can be rejuvenated by cutting all stems back to within 30cm (12in) of the ground in spring. If the shrub is exceptionally large and old, cut the stems 60–90cm (2–3ft) high. Heavy-duty, double-action loppers are usually needed (*above*). Alternatively, use a curved saw.

### WINTER COLOUR

Many shrubs are grown for their attractive stems which provide colour in winter months. These shrubs include the common dogwood (*Cornus alba*) and golden-twig dogwood (*C. stolonifera* 'Flaviramea'). In spring, cut down all stems to within 7.5cm (3in) of the ground. This encourages the development of fresh stems that will create a bright feature during winter.

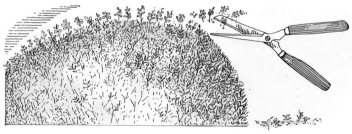

Use loppers or strong secateurs to cut stems of dogwoods to 7.5cm (3in) above their base.

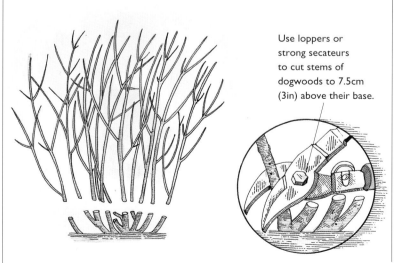

### TRIMMING HEATHERS

Keep heathers such as callunas, ericas and daboecias neat and tidy by trimming them with hand shears. Do not use secateurs, as these do not enable a contoured outline to be created. Trim callunas and summer-flowering ericas in spring, lightly clipping off the dead flowers and creating an undulating outline. However, take care not to cut into young shoots, as these will bear flowers later in the summer.

Trim winter- and spring-flowering ericas as soon as their flowers fade. Lightly brush off all the clippings – do not leave them on the plants.

Prune daboecias in late autumn, after flowering finishes. Lightly clip over them with hand shears to remove the old flower heads. In cold areas, however, leave this pruning until spring. At this time, any young shoots that subsequently develop will not be killed by frost.

# PRUNING TREES

Once established, both broad-leaved and coniferous trees need little pruning. During their early life, however, it is essential that conifers are checked every year to ensure they have only one leader shoot. If two are allowed to grow, the conifer develops a forked top. This is unsightly and in some areas heavy snowfalls make the tops of the conifers split. With most trees, once a framework of strong, well-spaced branches has been formed, there is little to do other than cutting out dead and diseased shoots and, occasionally, removing a low-growing branch – without spoiling the symmetry of the tree.

Trees are often expected to grow without receiving any attention from one year to another. Many will, but a regular inspection throughout the year will certainly extend a tree's life. Strong winds and heavy snowfalls break and bend branches. In winter, inspect trees and remove damaged, crossing or diseased branches. Some trees, such as members of the prunus family, should be cut only when their sap is rising, but most can be pruned in winter when they are dormant. It is easier to assess damage to deciduous trees in winter, when they are free from leaves. The pruning of many ornamental trees is detailed on pages 18 to 33.

Very old and prized trees may require more than just the removal of a branch. Branches may need to be propped up, while others may have cavities that need to be cleaned out and filled to prevent the decay spreading. This involves scraping back decayed wood to a sound base, painting the surface with a fungicidal wound-paint and then filling the cavity with bricks and sealing with cement. Provision must be made to ensure water seeping into the filled area can drain away.

**APPROPRIATE CHOICE**
Occasionally, the pruning a tree needs, once established, is a result of it becoming too large and intruding on other plants in a garden, or into a neighbour's territory. When choosing a tree, find out what its size will be after fifteen or twenty years.

There are trees of many shapes, sizes and degrees of vigour; a few create columns, while others have domed heads and some are cascading. No amount of pruning will encourage a weeping tree to be upright, and any that is done will only highlight the problem. In such cases it is best to remove the tree, renew the soil and plant one of more suitable habit.

**Removing a large branch**

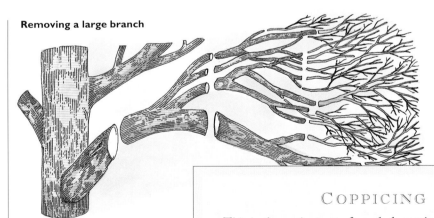

*1* When cutting off a large bough, remove it in several stages. Never cut it off close to the trunk in a single stage as the tree may be damaged. Cutting off a branch in several parts also creates pieces that are more manageable to move.

## COPPICING

This is the ancient art of regularly cutting down trees and shrubs to encourage the development of thin, pliable shoots from their bases, which are known as stools. Many young, broad-leaved trees can be coppiced to form dense thickets of shoots that can be harvested when they reach the desired thickness. Coppicing is best performed in late winter or early spring. Willow is very prolific when coppiced.

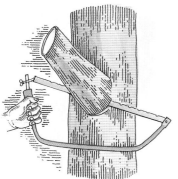

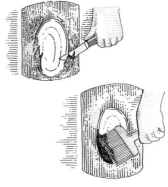

2 After a large branch has been cut back to about 45cm (18in) from the trunk, use a saw to cut two-thirds of the way through it from below. Position the cut close to the trunk, but not so near that it scrapes the bark. Making the first cut under the bough ensures that bark below the branch does not subsequently become damaged.

3 Cut through the remaining part of the branch from above. Position the saw so that the two cuts align and do not create a step. If they do not quite meet, use a coarse file to level them. If the two cuts are a long way out of alignment, it may be necessary to make a further cut to create a flat surface. Use a sharp saw – it makes the job easier.

4 Use a sharp knife to smooth the edges of the cut. If left rough, the cut both looks unattractive and extends the time the wound takes to heal. When smooth, coat the surface with a fungicidal wound-paint to prevent diseases entering the tree and eventually causing extensive damage to the trunk.

## POLLARDING

Trees in towns and cities often become too large for the area in which they were planted. Also, where roads are widened, overhanging branches may obstruct traffic. If this happens, branches are often cut back to the trunk, encouraging the growth of long stems that cluster around the top of the trunk. Pollarding can be avoided by selecting trees that will not intrude on neighbouring buildings, roads or gardens. Always select a species and variety to suit the position.

## SUPPORTING OLD TREES

As trees age, large branches often need to be supported, either by props placed underneath them or by giant, threaded, staple-like hooks secured by washers and nuts and then held by cables suspended from branches higher up.

In the past large, dog-collar-like constructions of iron were bolted around a limb that needed support and, by means of an iron rod or chain, linked to a similar device on a higher branch. Apart from being cumbersome and not pleasant to look at, the two 'dog-collars' eventually restrict the flow of sap to the ends of branches. The areas on either side of the band become swollen and, later, the branch has to be completely removed. Unless these bands can be adjusted every year, it is better to use props or staple-like hooks.

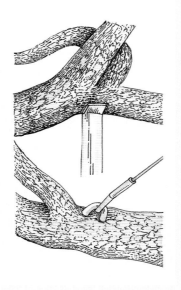

**RETAINING SYMMETRY**
Evergreen conifers with a symmetrical outline need little attention once established, but during their early years ensure that only one central shoot is allowed to develop. Use sharp secateurs to cut out one of the forked shoots. If the conifer is young, temporarily tie the leading shoot to a cane.

ABOVE Groupings of variously shaped and coloured evergreen conifers create attractive features throughout the year.

# A TO Z OF TREES AND SHRUBS

Within this section on pruning, shrubs and trees – including conifers as well as bamboos – are arranged alphabetically under their botanical names. Common names are also included. Some of these woody plants are evergreen, whereas others are deciduous or semi-evergreen, depending on the severity of the climate.

Nature has produced shrubs and trees with such a wide range of habits that it is not too surprising that pruning techniques vary widely, both in the time of year pruning is best performed and the type of shoots which are removed. Frequently plants within the same genus have different needs. For example, the horse chestnut family (*Aesculus*) is mainly formed of trees, usually too large for planting in gardens, but the bottlebrush buckeye (*Aesculus parviflora*) has a suckering nature, with shoots growing from ground level. With this species, encouraging the development of fresh shoots from ground level is important, whereas species grown as trees need little pruning other than being shaped when young.

**Abelia × grandiflora** No regular pruning is required. Simply cut out congested shoots in autumn to encourage the development of fresh growth. Twiggy and congested shoots on deciduous species are best cut out in early or mid-spring.

**Abeliophyllum distichum** An early-flowering shrub that needs little pruning, other than the cutting out of dead shoots in spring. In cold areas, leave pruning until early summer.

**Abies (silver fir)** Little pruning, other than ensuring young plants do not have two leading shoots. In spring, use sharp secateurs to remove one of the shoots, as well as sideshoots near the leader shoot.

**Abutilon megapotamicum (trailing abutilon)** Cut out frost-damaged and straggly shoots in mid-spring.

RIGHT Snowy mespilus (*Amelanchier lamarckii*) creates a feast of pure white, star-like flowers in large, loose clusters in mid-spring. In autumn, the green leaves, which are coppery when young, assume rich yellow and orange tints. Additionally, in late summer it develops red fruits that slowly become purple or black. It eventually forms a shrub up to 3m (10ft) high.

*Acer palmatum* 'Dissectum Atropurpureum' has deeply dissected, deep-red leaves and a domed, slightly pendulous outline, about 75cm (2¹/₂ft) high and 1.5m (5ft) wide.

*Acer japonicum* 'Aureum', a yellow-leaved form of the Japanese maple, is slow-growing and eventually 4.5–6m (15–20ft) high. In autumn, the leaves assume rich crimson tints before falling.

LEFT *Abutilon indicum* 'Kentish Belle' creates a magnificent display of bell-shaped flowers. Other abutilons include *A. megapotamicum*, which bears pendulous flowers in a combination of red and yellow and is best planted against a warm, sunny wall, where it grows about 1.8m (6ft) high. The form 'Variegatum' has beautiful yellow mottled leaves.

**Abutilon vitifolium** and **A.indicum** Prune in the same way as for *A. megapotamicum*.

**Acer japonicum (Japanese maple)** Prune to shape when young and occasionally remove congested shoots. Always prune in late summer or early autumn to prevent bleeding.

**Acer palmatum** It is the small forms with dissected leaves that are widely grown in gardens. Prune them lightly and in the same way as for *A. japonicum*.

**Aesculus parviflora (bottlebrush buckeye)** This is a suckering shrub. Cut out congested, old stems at ground level in late summer or early autumn to encourage the development of fresh ones. If pruning is left until spring there is a risk that the plant will bleed. This applies to all members of the well-known horse chestnut family.

**Amelanchier lamarckii (snowy mespilus)** Little pruning is needed, but thin out overcrowded bushes in early summer, after the flowers fade. *A. canadensis* and *A. laevis* are pruned in the same manner.

**Andromeda polifolia (bog rosemary)** Occasionally, cut out old stems after the flowers fade, in early summer.

**Aralia elata (Japanese angelica tree)** No regular pruning is needed, but if it spreads excessively, cut out shoots to ground level in spring.

**Araucaria araucana (monkey puzzle tree)** No pruning is needed, as invariably it spoils this conifer's outline.

**Arbutus** No regular pruning is needed, other than to cut out straggly shoots in spring. Also, cut out branches that obscure the trunks of trees grown for their attractive bark.

**Arctostaphylos uva-ursi (red bearberry)** No pruning is needed, as it dislikes being cut. Just nip out the tips of young plants during spring to encourage bushiness.

**Artemisia abrotanum (lad's love/southernwood)** Cut out frosted and congested shoots in early spring.

**Artemisia arborescens** Prune this deciduous or evergreen species in the same way as *A. abrotanum*.

***Arundinaria* (bamboo)** No regular pruning is needed, but when clumps become congested cut down old and exhausted canes to ground level in late spring. Heavy snowfalls can bend over the canes: any that are badly damaged should be cut out at ground level. However, damage can often be prevented by quickly removing the covering of snow.

***Aucuba japonica* 'Variegata' (spotted laurel/gold-dust tree)** No regular pruning is needed, but overgrown specimens can be cut back in spring to about 60cm (2ft) above the ground. The edges of leaves sometimes become blackened and singed by frost. In spring, cut back stems bearing damaged leaves.

**Azalea** No regular pruning is needed, but if bushes become congested, cut out a few old stems immediately after the flowers have faded.

**Azara** This range of Chilean evergreen shrubs, slightly tender in temperate regions, does not need regular pruning. However, if shoots are damaged by frost or become 'leggy', cut stems hard back in late spring, after all of the flowers have faded.

**Bamboo** See *Arundinaria*.

***Berberis*** No regular pruning is needed. If bushes become congested, cut back old or exhausted shoots to ground level or healthy main shoots. Prune deciduous types in late winter or early spring, when the beauty of their berries is over: prune evergreen varieties after their flowers fade.

***Betula* (birch)** No regular pruning is needed. Where a misplaced branch needs to be removed, cut it out in late autumn when there is less chance of it bleeding.

***Buddleia alternifolia*** As soon as the flowers fade in the latter part of early summer, cut back by two-thirds all stems that produced flowers. This prevents the shrub becoming congested with old shoots.

LEFT Bamboos create fascinating features in gardens and are ideal screening plants. *Arundinaria japonica*, grows up to 3.6m (12ft) high and has dark-green, sharply pointed leaves and olive-green canes which eventually form large thickets. Other beautiful species include *A. nitida*, which has purple-flushed canes up to 3m (10ft) high and bright-green leaves, and *A. murielae*, which has bright-green canes up to 2.4m (8ft) high, maturing to dull yellowish green, and dark-green leaves.

LEFT AND BELOW The Common Camellia (*Camellia japonica*) has a large number of varieties which create a wealth of flowers from late winter to late spring in colours including white, pink, red and purple. Some are single flowers, others semi-double, double, paeony – or anemone-shaped.

Spotted laurel (*Aucuba japonica* 'Variegata') remains attractive throughout the year. The shiny, dark-green, leathery leaves are irregularly peppered with yellow spots. Sometimes, this shrub is listed in catalogues as *A. j.* 'Maculata'.

Darwin's berberis (*Berberis darwinii*) is a hardy evergreen shrub from Chile. Its glossy, dark-green, holly-like leaves become hidden during late spring and early summer by pendulous yellow and orange flowers. These are followed by blue berries. It grows about 2.4m (8ft) high, except the 'Prostrata' variety which is much lower and well-suited for planting in small gardens.

***Buddleia davidii* (butterfly bush)** Regular pruning in early spring is essential: cut back all the previous season's shoots to within 5–7.5cm (2–3in) of the older wood. This encourages the development of fresh shoots that will bear flowers later in the same year.

***Buddleia globosa*** Prune immediately after the flowers fade in early summer. Cut out dead flowers, and 5–7.5cm (2–3in) of the old wood.

***Bupleurum fruticosum*** Cut back shoots fairly hard in late winter or early spring. This encourages the development in late spring and early summer of fresh, young shoots.

***Caesalpinia*** Shorten overly long shoots in late winter.

***Callicarpa*** During early and mid-spring, thin out overcrowded bushes, retaining as much of the young, healthy wood as possible.

***Calluna vulgaris* (heather/ling)** Use secateurs to cut back long shoots in early spring. Alternatively, trim over them with garden shears to remove dead flowers immediately they fade.

***Calycanthus* (allspice)** During spring, thin out overcrowded bushes, taking care to retain as much of the young and healthy wood as possible.

***Camellia*** No regular pruning is needed, other than shortening long shoots in mid-spring to produce well-shaped bushes. Plants that are old, with bare stems and bases, can be induced to produce further shoots by cutting them back by a third to a half of their height in mid-spring.

***Caragana arborescens* (Siberian pea tree)** No regular pruning is required, other than carefully shortening long growths on young plants after the flowers fade.

***Carpenteria californica*** Shorten long, straggly and weak shoots after the flowers fade in mid- to late summer.

***Caryopteris × clandonensis* (bluebeard)** In early spring, cut back shoots produced during the previous year – weak shoots to soil level and stronger ones to healthy buds. This encourages the development of fresh shoots from ground level.

***Cassinia*** Prune these heath-like shrubs in early spring to keep them shapely; shorten the longest stems.

LEFT *Buddleia alternifolia* creates a waterfall of sweetly scented, lavender-blue flowers on arching stems during early summer. It is usually grown as a shrub, but occasionally as a tree; in this form it is ideal for planting as a focal point in a lawn.

This shrubby plumbago (*Ceratostigma willmottianum*) is a slightly tender deciduous shrub, which creates a feast of small, rich-blue flowers in terminal clusters during mid- and late summer. It has the additional quality of bearing diamond-shaped, dark-green leaves that assume reddish tints in autumn.

*Cercis chinensis* is pruned in exactly the same way as the Judas tree (*C. siliquastrum*). It has a wealth of bright-pink, pea-type flowers in late spring and early summer and is ideal for planting as a focal point in a large lawn. The bare trunk, often up to about 1.2m (4ft) high, enables bulbous plants to be successfully grown under it.

### Ceanothus (Californian lilac)

Prune spring-flowering evergreen types, when grown as bushes, after their flowers fade. Shorten the longest shoots to keep the plant neat and shapely. But when evergreen varieties are grown against walls, cut back strong sideshoots to 2.5–5cm (1–2in) from the main branches as soon as flowering is over. Prune late summer- and autumn-flowering deciduous types in spring: cut out thin shoots and prune strong stems that produced flowers during the previous year to 15–30cm (6–12in) from the old wood.

### Cedrus (cedar)

No regular pruning needed, but ensure there is only one leading shoot. Cut off old branches in late winter or early spring, but take care not to spoil the conifer's outline.

### Ceratostigma willmottianum (shrubby plumbago/Chinese plumbago)

In temperate regions, shoots are often killed by frost. If this happens, cut the whole plant to ground level in mid-spring to produce new stems and flowers. If shoots are not damaged by frost, just cut out old, flowered ones.

### Cercis siliquastrum (Judas tree)

No regular pruning is needed, other than shaping when the plant is young and, later, removing dead shoots in spring when mature.

### Chaenomeles (Japanese quince/cydonia)

Plants grown as bushes in borders require little attention, except the removal of thin and congested shoots after the flowers have faded.

Californian lilacs (*Ceanothus*) are well-known for their clouds of blue flowers. Some of these floriferous shrubs are evergreen, others deciduous. Most evergreen types (shown here) flower in early summer, while the deciduous ones create their display from mid-summer and into early autumn.

The sweet pepper bush (*Clethra alnifolia*), native to North America, forms a deciduous shrub with fragrant, bell-shaped, creamy-white flowers during late summer and into autumn. Here is featured the pink-flowered 'Pink Spire'.

RIGHT The stems of *Chaenomeles speciosa* 'Cardinalis' are smothered in crimson-scarlet flowers during late winter and spring.

Mexican orange blossom (*Choisya ternata*) produces a wealth of white, sweetly scented, orange-blossom-like flowers mainly in late spring and early summer, then intermittently until autumn. The evergreen, glossy, dark-green leaves have an orange-like bouquet when crushed. Most gardens can accommodate this slightly tender shrub, which thrives in a warm, wind-sheltered corner and forms a dome about 1.5m (5ft) high.

*Chamaecyparis* **(false cypress)** No regular pruning is needed, but ensure leading shoots do not fork. Prune in mid-spring.

*Chimonanthus praecox* **(winter sweet)** When grown as bushes in a border, little attention is needed other than thinning shoots in spring. However, when grown against a wall, cut out flowered shoots to within two buds of their base after their yellow, spicy-scented flowers have faded.

*Chionanthus* **(fringe tree)** After the flowers fade, during mid-summer, thin crowded bushes by cutting out weak and spindly shoots.

*Choisya ternata* **(Mexican orange blossom)** No regular pruning is needed, other than pruning out straggly shoots after the first flush of flowers has faded. Also, cut out frost-damaged shoots in spring. Rejuvenate old bushes by cutting them hard back in late spring, but this means losing the subsequent summer's flowers.

*Cistus* **(rock rose)** During their infancy, nip out the growing points from young shoots to encourage the development of bushy plants. When fully grown these plants dislike being pruned: if old wood is cut, fresh shoots do not develop from it. Old, leggy, unsightly plants are best dug up and replaced.

*Clerodendriun trichotomum* and *C. bungei* **(glory bower)** These slightly tender shrubs need little pruning, other than cutting out the tips of any frost-damaged shoots in spring. When plants become large, cut them to within 30–38cm (12–15in) of their base in spring.

*Clethra alnifolia* **(sweet pepper bush)** and *C. arborea* **(lily-of-the-valley tree)** No regular pruning is needed, other than cutting out old shoots and removing thin and weak wood during winter and early spring.

*Colutea arborescens* **(bladder senna)** Completely cut out weak, twiggy and thin shoots in early spring. Cut back strong shoots to within a few buds of the old wood.

*Cornus* **(dogwoods)** The tree forms need no regular pruning, other than occasionally cutting them back in late winter to prevent intrusion on neighbouring plants. *C. alba* and *C. stolonifera*, which are frequently grown for their attractive young stems, should be cut to within 5cm (2in) of the ground in spring.

*Corylopsis* **(winter hazel)** No regular pruning is needed, other than occasionally thinning out crowded shoots after the flowers have faded.

*Corylus maxima* **'Purpurea' (purple-leaved filbert)** and *C. avellana* **'Aurea'** In late winter or early spring, cut back vigorous shoots to encourage the development of fresh shoots and attractive leaves.

**Cotoneaster** No regular pruning is needed. Just thin out the congested shoots on deciduous types in late winter, and on evergreen ones in mid- to late spring.

**Cryptomeria (Japanese cedar)** No regular pruning is needed, but ensure plants do not develop two leading shoots. Prune one of them out in spring.

× **Cupressocyparis leylandii (Leyland cypress)** Once plants are established with a single leading shoot, little further pruning is needed. If necessary to control size, prune in spring.

**Cupressus (cypress)** No regular pruning is needed, other than to ensure there is only one leading shoot. Prune in spring.

**Cytisus (broom)** Ensure young plants become bushy by trimming off leading shoots during their first summer. When established, prune plants that flower on the previous season's shoots as soon as the flowers have faded, removing two-thirds off all shoots. Plants which flower on the current season's growth are pruned in spring, cutting shoots hard back before growth recommences.

**Daboecia cantabrica (St Daboecia's heath)** Use garden shears to clip off dead flowers in late autumn, after the flowers have faded. In cold areas leave pruning this ericaceous plant until spring.

**Daphne** No regular pruning is needed, other than occasionally removing straggly shoots in spring.

The Warminster broom (Cytisus × praecox) has a bushy, vigorous habit, often 1.8m (6ft) high and with arching stems bearing creamy-white, pea-shaped flowers during mid- and late spring. The form 'Allgold' has bright-yellow flowers. When in flower it looks spectacular. Unfortunately, the flowers have a rather acrid smell.

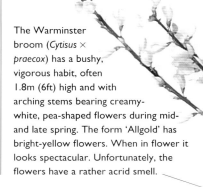

LEFT *Elaeagnus pungens* 'Goldrim' forms a bright evergreen shrub. The form 'Maculata' is another popular type, with leathery, glossy-green leaves splashed in gold. These forms of elaeagnus are ideal for brightening borders in winter and can be planted in full sun or light shade. 'Variegata' has creamy edges to its leathery leaves.

RIGHT Golden Bells (*Forsythia*) is one of the joys of spring. There are several species and varieties to choose from, but *F.* × *intermedia* 'Spectabilis' is one of the best, with bright-yellow, bell-shaped flowers. 'Lynwood' has even larger, rich-yellow flowers.

Garland flower (*Daphne cneorum*) is a prostrate, evergreen shrub, up to 15cm (6in) high and spreading to 90cm (3ft), with sweetly scented rose-pink flowers during late spring and early summer. There is also a white form, while 'Eximia' has large flowers, crimson when in bud and opening to rose-pink.

**Desfontainea spinosa** No regular pruning is needed, other than occasionally cutting out shoots so that the plant fits its allotted position. These shoots are dark-green and holly-like, and ideal for adding to flower arrangements, rather than just discarding.

**Deutzia** Cut out all flowered shoots to their bases as soon as the flowers have faded, in mid-summer.

**Dipelta floribunda** After the flowers have faded in early or mid-summer, cut a few of the old stems to ground level to keep the bushes open and to encourage the development of further shoots.

**Elaeagnus** No regular pruning is needed, but cut out mis-placed and straggly shoots, and all-green shoots from variegated shrubs, in spring.

**Elsholtzia stauntonii (mint shrub)** In late winter, cut back fairly hard all shoots that flowered during the previous year. At the same time, cut out weak and twiggy growths.

**Enkianthus campanulatusa:** No regular pruning is required – just maintain its shape in late winter.

**Erica (heath/heather)** Use garden shears in spring to trim off dead flowers from summer-flowering types. Clip winter- and spring-flowering types as soon as their flowers fade (see page 15 for details).

**Escallonia** Little regular pruning is needed, other than occasional cutting back shoots in spring or as soon as their flowers have faded.

**Eucryphia** No regular pruning is needed for established shrubs and trees, but cut off the ends of shoots on young plants.

**Euonymus** Deciduous types need no regular pruning, although they are improved by thinning out and shortening shoots in late winter. Evergreen types can be pruned to shape in spring.

**Exochorda (pearl bush)** No regular pruning is required.

**Fabiana imbricata** To encourage a bushy shape, shorten long shoots as soon as the flowers have faded.

**Fatsia japonica (false castor oil plant/Japanese fatsia)** No pruning is necessary, unless to create a better shape. Prune during spring.

**Forsythia (golden bells)** Prune yearly after the flowers have faded in spring. Cut out straggly and misplaced shoots, and shorten long and vigorous stems. If pruning is neglected, the shrub becomes choked with old wood, reducing the number of flowering shoots.

ABOVE *Eucryphia cordifolia* forms an upright, evergreen tree about 3m (10ft) high and 2.1m (7ft) wide. During late summer and early autumn it bears 6cm (2¼in) wide white flowers amid leathery, dull-green leaves.

*Fothergilla* No regular pruning is needed, other than occasionally thinning out overcrowded and twiggy shoots after the flowers have faded in late spring or early summer.

*Fuchsia magellanica* (**hardy fuchsia**) Cut back all shoots to ground level in spring to encourage fresh shoots.

*Garrya elliptica* (**silk-tassel bush**) When grown as a bush it needs little pruning, other than occasionally cutting out a few shoots so that it retains an attractive shape. If grown as a wall shrub, cut back long, secondary shoots in spring.

*Gaultheria* No regular pruning needed, but cut back large plants in spring.

*Genista* (**broom**) No regular pruning needed, but encourage bushiness in young plants by nipping out the tips of shoots.

*Ginkgo biloba* (**maidenhair tree**) Do not prune, as it may cause shoots to die back.

*Griselinia littoralis* The only pruning needed is to cut out long or misplaced shoots in spring or late summer.

*Halesia* (**snowdrop tree/silver bell tree**) No regular pruning is needed, but shorten long shoots after the flowers have faded to create a bushy shape.

*Hamamelis* (**witch hazel**) No regular pruning is needed, but cut back straggly, diseased, crowded or crossing shoots in late winter or spring.

*Hebe* (**shrubby veronica**) No regular pruning is needed, other than cutting back frost-damaged or straggly shoots in late spring. Also, cut back shrubs that have become leggy during spring.

*Helianthemum nummularium* Shorten straggly shoots and cut off old flower heads as soon as the flowers have faded.

*Hibiscus syriacus* (**shrubby althaea/shrubby mallow**) No regular pruning is needed; shorten long shoots in spring.

LEFT *Fothergilla major* is a North American deciduous shrub, about 1.8m (6ft) high and 1.5m (5ft) wide, with sweetly scented, creamy-white, flowers like bottle-brushes, in late spring. In autumn, the dark-green leaves develop red or orange-yellow tints. *F. monticola* is similar but wider. It is ideal for positioning at the junction of paths.

ABOVE The Chinese witch hazel (*Hamamelis mollis*), up to 2.4m (8ft) high and wide, bears spider-like, sweetly scented golden-yellow flowers during winter. In autumn this deciduous shrub has mid-green leaves that assume yellow tints before falling.

Variegated hollies are superb for creating colour throughout the year. The common holly (*Ilex aquifolium*) has many attractive variegated forms. Some of them, such as 'Ferox Argentea', have leaves with both variegation and puckered, spiny surfaces.

*Hippophae rhamnoides* **(sea buckthorn)** No regular pruning is needed, but cut out straggly shoots in late summer.

*Hydrangea arborescens* **(hills of snow)** During late winter or early spring, cut back by a third to a half all shoots that produced flowers during the previous year.

*Hydrangea macrophylla* **(French hydrangea/mop-head hydrangea)** There are two forms of this deciduous shrub – Hortensia and Lacecaps. In late winter or early spring, cut out to their bases all shoots that produced flowers during the previous year (see page 13). The old flower heads are removed in autumn, but leaving them in place until spring helps to provide protection for the plant when it is grown in a cold climate.

*Hydrangea paniculata* In late winter or early spring, cut back by a half all shoots that flowered during the previous year. If shoots are cut back by two-thirds, larger flower heads are produced, but the shrub's life may be reduced.

*Hypericum* **(St John's wort)** During late winter or early spring, shorten the previous season's strong flowering shoots by a quarter of their length. *H. calycinum* (rose of Sharon) can be cut down to within a few inches of ground level in early or mid-spring every few years to keep it compact.

*Ilex* **(holly)** No regular pruning is needed, other than cutting them to shape in spring. Excessively large or straggly shrubs can be cut back hard in late spring.

*Indigofera* **(indigo)** No regular pruning is needed, but cut out frost-damaged shoots in early spring. If shrubs become overcrowded and too large, or are severely damaged by frost, cut all shoots almost to ground level in late spring.

ABOVE *Hydrangea macrophylla* is a deciduous shrub, usually dome-shaped and 1.2–1.8m (4–6ft) high, with flowers from mid-summer to autumn. This form, Hortensia, has large, round flower heads. It needs regular pruning.

*Hypericum patulum* 'Hidcote' is a semi-evergreen shrub, usually about 90cm (3ft) high although sometimes slightly taller. From mid-summer to autumn it bears magnificent golden-yellow, saucer-like flowers.

*Magnolia* x *soulangeana* forms a spreading tree or large shrub bearing white, chalice-shaped flowers up to 15cm (6in) across during spring, before the leaves appear. Before opening, the flowers are stained rose-purple at their base.

ABOVE The beauty bush (*Kolkwitzia amabilis*) creates a magnificent display during late spring and early summer. Clusters of pink, foxglove-like flowers with yellow throats adorn the ends of twiggy stems. It has an upright stance, with arching branches, and grows 2.4–3m (8–10ft) high.

*Juniperus* (**juniper**) No pruning is needed, but ensure there is only one leading shoot.

*Kalmia* (**American laurel**) No regular pruning is needed, but cut off dead flowers.

*Kerria japonica* (**Jew's mallow/Japanese rose**) After the flowers have faded, cut out the old wood to strong, new growths. Alternatively, sever them at soil level to encourage the development of strong growths from the shrub's base.

*Kolkwitzia amabilis* (**beauty bush**) After the flowers have faded in early summer, completely cut out flowered shoots to encourage the development of fresh growth.

*Larix* (**larch**) No pruning is needed, but ensure each tree has only one leading shoot.

*Laurus nobilis* (**bay/laurel**) Specimen bushes and standards, in gardens and large tubs, need clipping with secateurs two or three times during summer. Rejuvenate neglected and old shrubs in late spring by cutting them back severely.

*Lavandula* (**lavender**) Use garden shears to clip over plants in late summer to remove dead flowers. Where plants have been neglected and become straggly, prune them hard back in spring. This encourages the development of shoots from the shrub's base.

*Ledum* No regular pruning is required for this genus.

*Leiophyllum buxifolium* (**sand myrtle**) No regular pruning is required for this species.

*Leycesteria formosa* (**granny's curls/Himalayan honey-suckle**) In spring, cut out to ground level all shoots that produced flowers during the previous year.

*Libocedrus decurrens* (**incense cedar**) Earlier known as *Calocedrus decurrens*, no pruning is needed except to ensure that only a single leading shoot is present.

**Lonicera nitida (Chinese honeysuckle/shrubby honeysuckle)** and **L. n. 'Baggesen's Gold'** When grown in borders, no pruning is needed. They can also be grown as hedges (*page 57*).

**Lupinus arboreus (tree lupin)** In late winter or early spring, remove old, worn-out stems and cut back to a quarter of their length strong growths that produced flowers during the previous year.

**Lycium barbatum (Duke of Argyll's tea/matrimony vine)** Occasionally thin out shoots in summer after the flowers have faded. Cut back any neglected and excessively large shrubs in spring.

**Magnolia** Deciduous types do not need pruning. Indeed, they resent being cut as wounds do not readily heal. However, prune the evergreen *M. grandiflora* in spring.

**Mahonia** No regular pruning is needed, but *M. aquifolium* (Oregon grape), when grown as ground-cover, can be cut hard back annually in spring.

**Malus (crab apple)** No regular pruning is needed, but ensure crossing, diseased, damaged or misplaced branches are cut out in late winter.

**Metasequoia glyptostroboides (dawn redwood)** No pruning needed, except to ensure that there is only one leading shoot.

**Neillia** No regular pruning is needed, but thin out congested growth in summer when the flowers have faded.

**Nyssa sylvatica (sour gum/ tupelo)** No pruning is needed.

**Olearia x haastii (daisy bush)** No regular pruning is needed, other than cutting out dead shoots and trimming and shaping plants in late spring or early summer.

**Osmanthus (devil-weed)** No regular pruning is needed, other than trimming to shape in spring.

**Paeonia suffruticosa (tree paeony)** No regular pruning is needed, other than cutting out dead shoots in spring and removing seed-pods as soon as the flowers fall.

**Pernettya mucronata** No regular pruning is needed, but old plants that become leggy can be severely cut back in late winter or early spring to encourage the development of fresh shoots.

**Perovskia atriplicifolia (Russian sage)** In mid-spring, cut all shoots to 30cm (12in) high. This encourages the development of fresh shoots. In cold areas, leave pruning until all risk of severe frost has passed.

**Philadelphus (mock orange)** After the flowers fade, cut out all shoots that produced flowers. Leave young shoots, as these will produce flowers during the following year.

**Phillyrea** No regular pruning is needed, other than shaping the shrub in mid-spring.

**Phyllostachys (bamboo)** See *Arundinaria* on page 20.

**Picea (spruce)** No regular pruning is needed, other than ensuring there is just one leading shoot.

**Pieris** Remove dead flowers. At the same time, cut out straggly shoots.

BELOW *Pieris japonica* 'Blush' is ideal for bringing colour to gardens in spring – particularly if the soil is moist and free from lime. It is slow-growing, eventually reaching 1.8m (6ft) high, with flowers that open from rose, when in bud, to pale blue-pink. 'Variegata' has green leaves edged in creamy-white.

The Jew's Mallow (*Kerria japonica*) is better known in North America as the Japanese rose. During late spring and early summer it develops yellow-orange flowers. The form 'Pleniflora' (also known as 'Flore-plena') has double flowers up to 5cm (2in) wide and is commonly known as batchelor's buttons. The double-flowered form is slightly more vigorous than the single type, but both are usually 1.2–1.8m (4–6ft) high.

**Pinus (pine)** No pruning is needed, except to ensure that there is only one leading shoot. Should the central shoot become damaged, remove all but the strongest from the growth below.

**Piptanthus laburnifolius (evergreen laburnum)** No regular pruning is needed, other than cutting back frost-damaged shoots to sound wood in early summer after the flowers have faded.

**Pittosporum** Shorten long, straggly shoots in late spring or early summer.

**Potentilla arbuscula** and **P. fruticosa (five-finger/ shrubby cinquefoil)** These shrubby plants need little pruning, other than cutting out straggly, old and weak shoots at their bases after the flowers have faded.

BELOW  The Tree Poppy (*Romneya coulteri*) –better known in North America as matilija poppy and Californian tree poppy – creates a magnificent display from mid-summer to autumn. It has a shrubby stance, but in very cold areas is more of a herbaceous plant, its foliage dying down in winter. *R. c. trichocalyx* is similar but more upright.

**Prunus** This family includes a wide range of ornamental shrubs and trees. They vary in the treatment required.

**Ornamental almonds (deciduous)** No regular pruning is needed, but cut back the old, flowered shoots of *P. glandulosa* and *P. triloba* immediately after their flowers have faded, trimming them to within two or three buds of the previous season's wood.

**Ornamental cherries (deciduous)** No regular pruning is needed, but if large branches need to be removed do this in late summer. When *P. incisa* (Fuji cherry) is grown as a hedge, however, it must be clipped immediately after its flowers fade.

**Ornamental peaches (deciduous)** No regular pruning is needed.

**Ornamental plums (deciduous)** No regular pruning is required, but hedges of *P. × blireana*, *P. × cistena* and *P. cerasifera* can be clipped at any time when not flowering.

**Ornamental cherry laurels (evergreen)** Use secateurs to cut back large plants in late spring or early summer.

ABOVE  Shrubby cinquefoils (*Potentilla arbuscula* and *P. fruticosa*) have a long flowering period, from early summer to autumn. There are many varieties, in colours including yellow, tangerine-orange and red. Here is 'Moonlight'.

Japanese Cherries swamp gardens with colourful blossom in spring. One of the best known of these cherries is *Prunus* 'Kanzan', famed for its coppery-red, young leaves and purple-pink, double flowers which are borne in large clusters. It is vigorous and eventually forms a large tree.

The Bird Cherry (*Prunus padus* 'Watereri'), sometimes known as 'Grandiflora', develops almond-scented white flowers in tail-like clusters up to 20cm (8in) long during late spring and into early summer. Eventually it forms a large tree, about 7.5m (25ft) high and 6m (20ft) wide and therefore needs plenty of space. Plant it where the fragrance, flower shape and colour can be easily admired.

Rhododendrons and azaleas are the epitome of late spring- and early summer-flowering shrubs in soils free from lime. Some rhododendrons, however, flower in mid-winter, others during late summer. Nevertheless, where there is a slight slope, with a high overhead canopy of pines or other coniferous trees, they will create a spectacular display. Rhododendrons and azaleas illustrated here include (clockwise from the extreme left) 'Sappho', 'Percy Wiseman', 'Lili Marlene', 'Red Bird' and 'Purple Spendor'.

*Pyracantha* **(firethorn)** Shrubs grown in borders need little pruning, other than cutting them to shape in late spring or early summer – but avoid cutting off flowers. When grown against a wall, shorten long sideshoots in mid-spring, but take care not to cut off too many that would subsequently bear flowers. When wall shrubs become too vigorous, cut them back to old wood in spring, although it means sacrificing the season's flowers.

*Pyrus salicifolia* 'Pendula' **(willow-leaved pear)** No regular pruning is needed, but occasionally thin out overcrowded branches and shorten long, straggly growths in late summer.

*Rhamnus* **(buckthorn)** During late spring, thin out old wood on evergreen types to keep them shapely and to ensure light and air can reach the shrub's centre. Prune deciduous species in winter.

*Rhododendrons* No regular pruning is needed, other than to cut back frost-damaged shoots in spring. Where plants are leggy and large, cut them back in mid-spring, if necessary to about 30cm (12in) above the soil.

*Rhus* **(sumac/sumach)** Usually, no regular pruning is needed, but if a mass of foliage is required cut all stems of *R. typhina*, *R. t.* 'Laciniata' and *R. glabra* to the ground each year between late winter and mid-spring. In cold areas, leave pruning until late spring.

*Ribes* **(flowering currant)** Annually, cut out all old wood to ground level in late spring.

*Romneya* **(Matilija poppy/tree poppy)** These sub-shrubby perennials need little pruning, other than cutting out frost-damaged shoots in mid-spring.

*Rosa* **(rose)** See pages 60 to 73.

*Rosmarinus officinalis* **(rosemary)** Cut out dead shoots in spring and shorten the tips of long, straggly shoots. If plants become overcrowded, cut them back in mid-spring.

*Rubus* **(ornamental brambles)** During late spring, cut to ground level all old stems on those species grown for their coloured stems. This will encourage the development of fresh ones. For others, cut to ground level a few of the old stems as soon as the flowers have faded.

*Ruscus aculeatus* **(butcher's broom)** No regular pruning is needed, except for cutting out dead shoots in spring. If neglected, this shrub becomes clogged with old, dead shoots.

*Salix* **(osier/willow)** No regular pruning is needed for the tree forms, other than occasionally cutting out dead shoots during winter. However, several species are grown for their coloured stems, such as *S. alba* 'Chermesina' and 'Vitellina', and these are completely cut back to within 5–7.5cm (2–3in) of the ground in late winter or early spring.

*Sambucus* **(elder)** Thin out bushes in mid-spring to keep them neat and shapely. Where forms such as *S. racemosa* 'Plumosa Aurea' and *S. nigra* 'Aurea-variegata' are grown for their colourful leaves, cut all the stems back to ground level each spring.

*Santolina chamaecyparissus* Lightly clip off old flowers with hand shears, as soon as they fade. Rejuvenate old plants by cutting them hard back in late spring.

*Sarcococca* **(sweet box)** When shrubs become crowded, cut out a few of the old stems to ground level after the flowers have faded.

*Sasa* **(bamboo)** See *Arundinaria* on page 20.

*Skimmia* No regular pruning is needed, but shorten long, straggly shoots in spring.

*Sorbus* **(mountain ash)** No regular pruning is needed. Thin out or shape trees in winter after the fruits have fallen. Additionally, cut out obstructive branches that have become too low.

RIGHT The bridal wreath (*Spiraea × arguta*) becomes smothered in 5cm (2in) wide clusters of white flowers during mid- and late spring. It is a superb deciduous shrub, ideal for shrub borders as well as alongside paths and boundaries. Other spring-flowering species including *S. thunbergii*, with 2.5cm (1in) wide clusters of white flowers, and *S. vanhouttei* with dense clusters of white flowers during early summer.

***Spartium junceum* (Spanish broom)** Lightly trim young plants several times during summer to encourage bushiness. When established, shorten stems to a third or half of their length in late winter or early summer. Trimming this shrub in autumn is frequently claimed to encourage the development of early flowers.

***Spiraea × arguta* (bridal wreath/foam of May)** On young and semi-mature shrubs, cut back flowering shoots as soon as the flowers have faded, leaving one or two young shoots at the base of each shoot. As a shrub develops, cut out as much of the old wood as possible in late winter, leaving the previous year's growth to produce flowers during the current year.

***Spiraea × bumalda* and *S. japonica*** Prune all stems to within 7.5–10cm (3–4in) of the ground in late winter or early spring.

***Spiraea thunbergii*** Prune in the same way as for *S. × arguta*.

***Spiraea × vanhouttei*** Prune in the same way as for *S. × arguta*.

***Stachyurus*** No regular pruning is needed, but occasionally shorten long shoots in mid-spring to maintain the shrub's shape.

***Staphylea* (bladdernut)** No regular pruning is needed, but occasionally cut back long growths after the flowers have faded in late spring.

***Stephanandra*** Cut out old and spindly shoots in late winter or early summer.

***Stransvaesia*** No regular pruning is needed, other than occasionally cutting out crowded shoots in spring.

The double-flowered gorse (*Ulex europaeus* 'Plenus') is evergreen, with scale-like leaves on stems drenched in double, bright-yellow, pea-like flowers during spring. Flowers often continue to appear, intermittently, throughout summer and occasionally until late winter.

RIGHT *Spartium junceum*, the Spanish broom, is a hardy deciduous shrub with rush-like stems that bear golden-yellow, pea-like, fragrant flowers from early to late summer. Well-drained soil and plenty of sun are essential to its growth.

Lilac creates eye-catching, pyramidal spires of flowers, mainly in spring and early summer. The range of varieties is wide and includes white, pink and purplish-red, and in single- and double-flowered forms. Some of them are superbly scented.

*Symphoricarpos* **(snowberry)** During late winter, cut out a few of the oldest stems to ground level and cut out crowded stems.

*Syringa* **(lilac)** Each year, use secateurs to cut off faded flowers. Later, during winter, cut out weak and crossing branches. Where lilacs have been neglected, rejuvenate them by cutting the entire plant to 60–90cm (2–3ft) above the ground during mid-spring. However, it then takes the shrub two or three years to produce flowers. In summer it is necessary to cut off suckers growing from the main stem.

*Tamarix* **(tamarisk)** Prune the spring-flowering *T. tetrandra* immediately the flowers have faded. Cut back by half to two-thirds of the previous season's growth. Prune the late summer-flowering *T. pentandra* in late winter or early spring, again cutting back the previous season's shoots by half to two-thirds.

*Taxus* **(yew)** No regular pruning needed but clusters of sucker-like shoots should be cut from the tree's trunk. This can be done at any time.

*Thuja* **(arbor vitae)** No pruning is needed, but ensure there is only one leading shoot.

*Tsuga* **(hemlock)** No regular pruning is needed, but ensure there is only one leading shoot present on a tree.

*Ulex* **(gorse)** No regular pruning is needed, but tall, leggy plants can be cut back to within 15cm (6in) of the ground in early spring.

*Vaccinium* **(blueberry)** No regular pruning is needed, but deciduous species that become overcrowded can be pruned during late winter by cutting out old stems to soil level or to strong, young growths. Evergreen species are pruned to shape in mid- to late spring. See also pages 106 and 107.

*Viburnum* No regular pruning is needed for deciduous species, other than occasionally cutting out crowded branches after the flowers have faded. Prune winter-flowering types in spring, and summer-flowering ones in mid-summer, after the flowers have faded. Thin out evergreen types in spring.

*Weigela* Each year, after the flowers have faded in mid-summer, cut out to soil level a few of the old stems. If this is neglected, the shrub soon becomes a tangled web of old shoots that produce only small and inferior flowers.

RIGHT Weigela hybrids are deciduous shrubs with small, foxglove-like flowers during early summer. The hybrids grow 1.5–1.8m (5–6ft) high. In addition to varieties grown for their flowers, the form 'Variegata' has mid-green leaves with creamy-white edges. Here is 'Eva Rathke', with crimson flowers.

*Viburnum plicatum* 'Mariesii' creates a wealth of white flowers, borne in tiers, during late spring and early summer.

# CLIMBING PLANTS

Most gardens have space for climbing plants. Walls and fences can be brightened, while pergolas and rustic poles offer further decorative opportunities. Apart from glorious arrays of flowers, many climbers produce colourful leaves and berries in a feast of rich autumn hues. Deciduous climbers that create the best display of autumnal colour include the well-known Boston ivy (*Parthenocissus tricuspidata*) and the true Virginia creeper (*P. quinquefolia*). As well as being a feature in their own right, evergreen climbers also create backgrounds for other garden plants. A few climbers are vigorous enough to grow up through trees, where they can brighten what may be an old and unattractive feature.

As well as giving support for plants, some walls provide sheltered, sun-saturated places for shrubs with a leaning nature that are too tender to be planted in a border. There are also wall shrubs such as pyracantha that survive on exposed, cold walls in extremely cold temperate regions.

**CLIMBING TACTICS**

The nature of climbing plants varies widely; some have stickers and cling to brickwork with great ease, whatever its height. Others are leaners and need a wall or trellis to support them and to which they can be tied. Then there are stems with thorns that hook over supports, either trellises or trees, and scramble their way upwards. Others have tendrils that loop around their hosts. These different ways of climbing influence the supports and type of pruning needed. For instance, ivies tenaciously cling to walls and the only pruning necessary is to thin them out and to restrain their spread. Conversely, the winter-flowering jasmine (*Jasminum nudiflorum*) is a leaner and as well as having old, flowered stems removed also needs to have the new ones loosely tied to a supporting framework.

The nature of a climber influences where it is planted, what support it is given and

ABOVE The flannel bush or fremontia (*Fremontodendron californicum*, although often still known as *Fremontia californica*) is widely grown against a warm, sunny wall in temperate climates. From early to late summer it displays golden-yellow, slightly cup-shaped flowers about 5cm (2in) wide. OPPOSITE The white wisteria (*Wisteria floribunda* 'Alba') has a dramatic but demure nature.

the method of pruning. Understanding a climber's character is fundamental to growing it to perfection and for this reason all of the climbers mentioned in this section have their characters described. Most climbers have a permanent or yearly renewable framework of stems, and these 'woody' types are featured here. Others have a herbaceous nature and need only their old stems to be severed and removed at the end of the growing season. There are, of course, annual climbers, but as these do not require pruning – only support and initial guidance – they are not featured here.

In addition to climbers, many shrubs are ideal for growing against walls; a few of these shrubs are evergreen and create a permanent array of leaves, while others are deciduous and therefore are barren of colour in winter, a reflection of their less hardy nature.

# CLIMBING HABITS

Most woody, perennial climbers live for fifteen or more years, some a great deal longer. For some of them, longevity depends on regular pruning, cutting out old, congested and dead stems to encourage the development of fresh shoots. Part of the success in growing climbers is in providing them with suitable places to scale or surfaces to which they can cling. It is no good, for example, expecting a clematis to scale a wall without the provision of wires or a trellis; in such a position, self-clinging climbers such as ivies, true Virginia creeper (*Parthenocissus quinquefolia*) and Chinese Virginia creeper (*P. henryana*), are better. Clearly, before selecting a climber it is essential to find out about its nature and if a supporting framework is required. It may be thought that all climbers which are self-clinging and scale walls never need pruning, and that all of those which use tendrils to help them climb are pruned in the same way. Unfortunately, this is not so. The pruning of individual climbers is described on pages 40 to 47.

### HOW THEY CLIMB

Climbers are a disparate group, a conglomeration of plants from many parts of the world. Some of them are totally hardy in temperate regions, others are native to warmer areas and need hospitable homes against a warm, wind-sheltered wall. They can be arranged into four different groups:

✳ The first of these groups encompasses climbers with no visible means of support and they are considered to be nature's leaners. Examples of these are *Abutilon megapotamicum*, winter-flowering jasmine (*Jasminum nudiflorum*), Chilean potato tree (*Solanum crispum*) and, of course, roses, although many of these have large thorns that assist stems to latch on to supports. There are other leaners, including members of the bramble family.

✳ Climbers in the second group are entirely self-supporting, using adhesive discs or aerial roots to cling to surfaces. Ivies (*Hedera*), the Japanese climbing hydrangea (*Hydrangea anomala petiolaris*), the Chinese Virginia creeper (*Parthenocissus henryana*) and the True Virginia Creeper (*P. quinquefolia*) are examples of self-supporting types. The only pruning that is necessary with these climbers is to restrain them and occasionally to cut out dead shoots.

✳ The third group is formed of climbers that use tendrils to cling to their hosts or supports. All shrubby clematis are in this group, together with the common passion flower (*Passiflora caerulea*) and the vines in the grapevine family, including the Japanese crimson glory vine (*Vitis coignetiae*).

LEFT *Clematis armandii* is vigorous, grows up to 9m (30ft) high and creates a wealth of saucer-shaped white flowers during mid-and late spring. There are two excellent forms: 'Snowdrift' with large, pure white flowers, and 'Apple Blossom', which is white tinged with pink. It clings and scrambles, tends to be untidy and needs plenty of space. It is one of the few clematis that are evergreen.

ABOVE *Vitis coignetiae* (Japanese crimson glory vine) is especially vigorous when given a large building or tree to scale. It is often claimed to grow more than 18m (60ft) high. During autumn, the green leaves turn yellow, then orange-red and purple-crimson. No amount of pruning will constrain it to a small area and therefore only plant it where space is unlimited. It is ideal for clambering up a tree.

## DAMAGE TO WALLS AND GUTTERING

If not regularly inspected, climbers can damage walls and block guttering and drainpipes. Even shoots of wisteria are inquisitive and delve behind old and loose, simulated beams on the outsides of houses. Nevertheless, if climbers are checked every year, few buildings are harmed. The main problem is when both houses and climbers are neglected. Do not allow brick-hugging ivies to clamber up painted, pebble-dashed walls; when the surface needs repainting it is easier to remove a wooden trellis that is supporting a clematis than to have to pull off a well established ivy. For this reason, it is often better to grow climbers up garden walls, pergolas or free-standing trellises where they cannot damage the fabric of houses and become an expensive problem.

✱ The fourth group of climbers includes those that twine around their hosts, supporting themselves and often creating a mass of stems. These include; the kolomikta vine (*Actinidia kolomikta*); the common white jasmine (*Jasminum officinale*); the honeysuckle (*Lonicera periclymenum*); the Russian vine (*Polygonum baldschuanicum*, also known as *Fallopia baldschuanica*); and the wisterias.

RIGHT, BELOW *Lonicera periclymenum* 'Harlequin' is an attractively variegated form of the popular honeysuckle.

BELOW The mountain clematis (*Clematis montana*) is one of the best-known and most widely grown clematis, with a deciduous nature and pure white flowers up to 5cm (2in) wide during late spring and early summer. It is a climber that clings to its host by means of tendrils, its thickened stems helping to support the lower part. It is ideal for covering pergolas, trellises, fences and arbours.

### HOUSE SECURITY

Few gardeners consider the security implications when planting climbers against house walls. At one time, the only use of a climber – apart from its aesthetic qualities – was for juvenile pranksters to escape from bedrooms. Nowadays, unfortunately, strong-stemmed climbers, together with a wooden trellis, offer rapid access to the outside of an upstairs window when houses are not constantly attended.

Not all climbers, however, create good and secure footholds: small-leaved ivies such as *Hedera helix* 'Goldheart' will not give sufficient support, nor will large-leaved types like the Persian ivy (*Hedera colchica*) or the Canary Island ivy (*H. canariensis* 'Variegeta' or 'Gloire de Marengo') unless many years old and with a tangled nature. Neither are the large-flowered clematis hybrids nor the species types a security risk. Old, long-established wisterias, with thickened bases and well-established stems, create the biggest security risk, together with newly installed trellises that, if well secured to walls, are just like ladders. Old climbing roses may appear to offer easy access, but their thorn-clad stems do not make hospitable hand- and foot-holds. Also, their stems are whippy and not supportive.

If you have worries about house security, grow climbers only on pergolas, garden walls and free-standing trellises. Also, climbers such as roses can be encouraged to climb tall trees, while species clematis and large-leaved ivies can be used to clothe tree trunks.

# PRUNING CLIMBERS

Climbers comprise a medley of plants with a wide range of growing and flowering habits. Many need yearly pruning to encourage the development of flowers, while some can continue in an unpruned state until they reach a stage when renovation is essential (*see below*). Left to nature, of course, many climbers rely on their old and woody shoots to create support for new shoots. But gardeners are less tolerant of old, unproductive shoots and, where possible, like to remove them and provide climbers with artificial support. When constructing supports, ensure that stems can pass around both sides of vertical and horizontal rails. With pergolas and rustic poles this is always possible, but if a wooden trellis is secured to a wall it is essential that at least 25mm (1in) – and preferably 36mm (1½in) – is allowed between the framework and wall.

**RENOVATING A CLIMBER**
Eventually – and especially if neglected over several years – many climbers develop a tangled web of old wood. Slowly, the climber's ability to flower is diminished and it becomes full of congested, old, unflowering shoots. Renovating a climber is best performed in spring.

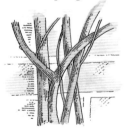

ABOVE Cut out as much of the old, congested growth as possible. Usually it is a matter of repeatedly snipping out small pieces of entangled shoots.

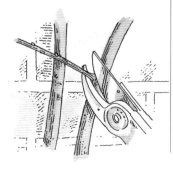

BELOW, LEFT Use sharp secateurs to cut out old, dead, twiggy shoots back to a healthy stem .
BELOW At the same time, cut back diseased shoots to strong and healthy shoots. If left, they will spread infection and disease.

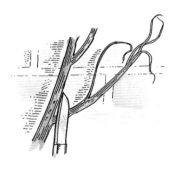

BELOW Some climbers continually develop new stems from their bases; the old ones eventually become thick, unproductive and congested. Use strong loppers to cut off these shoots at their base.

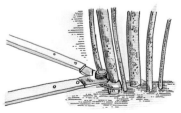

## RENOVATING HONEYSUCKLE

Even the name honeysuckle evokes thoughts of canopies and arbours drenched in fragrant flowers. Unfortunately, in many ways some honeysuckles – including the Japanese honeysuckle (*Lonicera japonica*), early Dutch honeysuckle (*L. periclymenum* 'Belgica') and late Dutch honeysuckle (*L. p.* 'Serotina') – are too undemanding for their own good, and will continue to flower for many years without having to be pruned. In time, however, the weight of their leaves and stems can often break their supports. If a climber does become a total mass of old stems, in spring cut the complete plant to within 38–50cm (15–20in) of the ground (BELOW, LEFT). Where it is just a mass of thin, tangled shoots, cut back the dead shoots from the base and use hand shears to trim thin shoots back to new growths (BELOW, RIGHT).

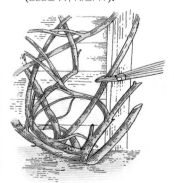

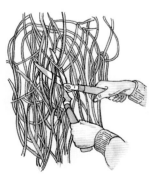

Use secateurs or loppers.          Trim with strong hand shears.

**Pruning young wisterias**

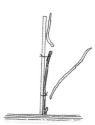

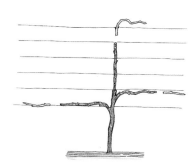

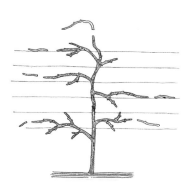

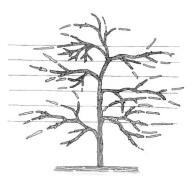

*1* Young wisterias need careful pruning and training to ensure a strong framework is created. During late winter or early spring in the year after being planted, cut back the strongest shoot to about 75cm (2½ft) above the ground. At the same time, completely cut off all other shoots.

*2* During mid-winter of the second year, cut back the central leading shoot to within 75–90cm (2½–3ft) of the topmost lateral shoot. At the same time, lower the laterals so that they are horizontal and cut them back by a third. Sever these lateral stems just beyond a bud on the upperside. Tie them to the wires.

*3* During winter of the third year, sever the central leading shoot to within 75–90cm (2½–3ft) of the uppermost horizontal stem. Then, lower the topmost horizontal shoots and cut them back by about a third. The lower horizontal shoots will have grown – cut off about a third of their new growth.

*4* In subsequent winters, continue forming new tiers of horizontal shoots, as well as encouraging the growth of the leader shoot. When the desired height is reached, cut it off fractionally above the uppermost horizontal shoot. At the same time, cut back sideshoots to within 7.5–10cm (3–4in) of their base.

## STANDARD WISTERIAS

Wisterias are usually trained over pergolas and rustic poles or against house walls. An alternative and unusual way is to train a single stem up a 1.8–2.1m (6–7ft) tall stake and then train branches over a wooden framework that radiates out and forms a flat-topped umbrella.

Start with a young plant and tie it to a strong stake. Train the shoot's tip upwards and at the same time allow sideshoots to develop – cut them back to about 23cm (9in) long. Later, when the central shoot is 45–60cm (1½–2ft) above the top of the supporting framework, cut it off and allow sideshoots at the top to develop to form a canopy. Later, cut off all of the other sideshoots, close to the main stem.

When established, both summer- and winter-pruning (*see right*) is necessary to ensure the regular production of flowers, and curb an excessive amount of growth.

## PRUNING ESTABLISHED WISTERIAS

Once a framework has been formed, the most important objective is to keep the climber in check – lateral shoots may grow up to 3.6m (12ft) in a single year and unless this growth is pruned the plant can soon become a jungle of stems and too large for its allotted area. Severely pruning a wisteria during winter will encourage even more rapid growth. However, by cutting it in summer it is possible to restrain the plant without encouraging massive growth.

In late or early winter, cut back all shoots to within two or three buds of the point where they started growing in the previous season. Where a plant becomes too large, also prune it in mid-summer, cutting the current season's young shoots back to within five or six buds of its base.

Summer-pruning

# PRUNING CLIMBERS AND WALL SHRUBS

*Abutilon* This slightly tender shrub is best grown in the protection of a warm wall. Shorten frost-damaged and straggly shoots in mid-spring. Tie main shoots to a wire or cane framework.

*Acacia* (wattle) In temperate regions, these Australian and Tasmanian shrubs flourish when planted against a warm, sheltered wall. Once the framework is formed, little attention is needed.

*Actinidia chinensis* (Chinese gooseberry/kiwi fruit) No regular pruning is needed, other than occasionally thinning out and trimming back long shoots in late winter. For more details on fruiting see page 107.

*Actinidia kolomikta* (kolomikta vine) Prune in the same way as for *A. chinensis* (*above*).

*Akebia* Little pruning is needed, other than cutting out excessively long or dead shoots in spring. It needs little training as the twining shoots soon clamber over supports.

*Ampelopsis* No regular pruning is needed, other than occasionally cutting out any dead or overcrowded shoots in spring.

*Aristolochia macrophylla* (Dutchman's pipe) Little pruning is needed, other than shortening excessively long shoots by one-third in late winter or early spring.

*Berberidopsis corallina* (coral plant) A slightly tender shrub best grown against a wall. No regular pruning is needed, other than cutting out dead shoots in late winter or early spring. Ensure this Chilean shrub is planted in a cool,

sheltered, slightly shaded position. The soil can be acid or neutral, and preferably light, well-drained and sandy.

*Campsis radicans* (trumpet vine) It is essential to cut back newly planted climbers to about 15cm (6in) high to encourage the development of shoots from the plant's base. Prune established plants in late winter or early spring, cutting shoots that were produced during the previous year to 5–7.5cm (2–3in) from the bases.

*Carpenteria californica* An evergreen shrub best grown against a warm wall. No regular pruning is needed, but cut out straggly shoots after the flowers have faded.

*Ceanothus* (Californian lilac) Many evergreen species and varieties grow best against a warm, sheltered wall. These include *C. rigidus*, *C. impressus*, *C.* × *burkwoodii* and *C.* 'Cascade' (*although see page 22*). Little pruning is needed, but shorten the previous year's growths in spring.

ABOVE The chocolate vine or five-leaved akebia (*Akebia quinata*) is a semi-evergreen climber, with leaves formed of five leaflets. During spring it develops dark-purple flowers, followed by dark-purple, sausage-shaped fruits. Even when not bearing flowers, this climber is very attractive.

ABOVE *Abutilon* x *suntense* is a garden hybrid with clusters of eye-catching violet-purple flowers from mid-spring to autumn. It grows to a height of 2m (6ft) with a spread of 1.5–2m (4–6ft).

RIGHT The trumpet vine (*Campsis radicans*) is a vigorous North American climber, where it is also known as cow-itch and trumpet honeysuckle. When given a warm, sheltered position it can grow up to 9m (30ft) high, but is usually smaller. It adheres to supports by its aerial roots. The light-green leaves have nine or eleven leaflets, with brilliant orange and scarlet flowers appearing in terminal clusters during late summer and autumn.

ABOVE Japanese quince (*Chaenomeles*) is a genus of three hardy, spring-flowering shrubs that grow well on banks or against walls. 'Cardinalis', shown here, is a raised garden form and has beautiful crimson to deep-red flowers.

*Celastrus orbiculatus* (**oriental bittersweet/staff vine**) When this climber is grown against a wall or on a pergola, thin out unwanted or misplaced shoots in early spring, and cut back main shoots by half. When it is growing up a tree, it can be left alone.

*Chaenomeles* (**Japanese quince/cydonia**) When planted against a wall, cut back the previous season's growths in spring or early summer, after the flowers have faded, to two or three buds of their base.

*Chimonanthus praecox* (**winter sweet**) When grown against a wall, cut out all flowered shoots to within two buds of their base after the flowers fade.

BELOW Oriental bittersweet (*Celastrus orbiculatus*), also known as staff vine and climbing bittersweet, grows up to 9m (30ft) high and during early and mid-summer reveals starry, greenish-yellow flowers. These are followed by glistening, orange-yellow fruits, while the leaves change from mid-green to clear yellow in autumn.

*Eccremocarpus scaber* (**Chilean glory flower**) In late spring cut out frost-damaged shoots. If the plant is severely damaged by frost, cut all stems to their bases in spring to encourage the development of fresh ones.

*Hedera canariensis* '**Variegata**' (**Canary Island ivy,** sometimes sold as '**Gloire de Marengo**') Plants are usually left to grow naturally, but if left completely alone for several years they may block gutters and penetrate cracks and crevices. Therefore, during late winter or early spring of every year, check and cut back invasive shoots. Also cut back long stems in late summer.

*Hedera colchica* '**Dentata Variegata**' (**variegated Persian ivy**) This evergreen climber has large leaves. Prune in the same way as recommended for *H. canariensis* 'Variegata'.

*Hedera helix* '**Goldheart**' This small-leaved ivy sometimes becomes invasive and dominates a wall. If this happens, prune it in the same way as for *H. canariensis* 'Variegata'. Several other varieties with attractive leaves can be pruned in the same way.

*Humulus lupulus* '**Aureus**' (**yellow-leaved or golden hop**) This climber is herbaceous and each year all stems die down to ground level. Fresh shoots appear in spring; remove dead shoots in late autumn or early winter.

*Hydrangea anomala petiolaris*, also known as *H. scandens* (**Japanese climbing hydrangea**) No regular pruning is needed, other than cutting out dead shoots in spring.

*Jasminum nudiflorum* (**winter-flowering jasmine**) After the flowers have faded in mid-spring, cut out to within 5–7.5cm (2–3in) of ground level all shoots that produced flowers. This encourages the development of fresh shoots. At the same time, cut out weak and old shoots completely.

BELOW *Hedera helix* 'Goldheart' is a superb small-leaved, variegated ivy for clambering up walls. The dull green leaves are irregularly splashed with yellow. It is self-supporting and needs little attention once established. When planted to scale a sunny wall it has a tendency to grow rapidly, but excess shoots can easily be removed in autumn.

LEFT Canary Island ivy (*Hedera canariensis* 'Variegata', but also known as *H. h.* 'Gloire de Marengo') is a popular evergreen climber which eventually forms a dense screen of large, dark-green leaves that merge to silvery-grey edged in creamy-white.

Variegated Persian ivy (*Hedera colchica* 'Dentata Variegata') is another evergreen climber, with pale-green oval or heart-shaped leaves about 20cm (8in) long, with creamy-yellow edges that later become creamy-white.

RIGHT Japanese climbing hydrangea (*Hydrangea anomala petiolaris*) is hardy and vigorous, reaching 12m (40ft) or more when given a large tree to climb. Normally it is less vigorous and looks superb when cascading up and over a high wall. During early summer it develops flat-headed clusters, up to 25cm (10in) wide, of creamy-white flowers.

The yellow-leaved hop (*Humulus lupulus* 'Aureus') is a superb herbaceous climber, with bright yellow leaves. It is ideal for creating a screen up to about 1.8m (6ft) high.

The early Dutch honeysuckle (*Lonicera periclymenum* 'Belgica') creates a mass of purple-red and yellow flowers during early and mid-summer. The late Dutch honeysuckle (*L. p.* 'Serotina') has reddish-purple flowers with creamy-white insides from mid-summer to autumn.

*Jasminum officinale* (**common white jasmine**) After the flowers have faded, thin out flowered shoots to their bases. Do not just shorten them.

*Jasminum polyanthum* In temperate regions this climber is usually grown indoors, but in mild areas it can be grown outdoors and against a warm, wind-sheltered wall. No regular pruning is needed, except occasionally to thin out overgrown plants and to cut out dead shoots after the flowers have faded.

*Lapageria rosea* (**Chilean bell flower**) It is only half-hardy in temperate regions and therefore must be planted against a warm, sunny wall. After the flowers have faded in late summer or early autumn, thin out weak growths.

*Lonicera japonica* (**Japanese honeysuckle**) No regular pruning is needed, other than occasionally thinning out congested plants in spring. See page 38 for renovating old and large honeysuckles.

*Lonicera japonica* '**Aureoreticulata**' This is susceptible to frosts and may lose its leaves. No regular pruning is needed, other than occasionally thinning out old shoots after the flowers fade.

*Lonicera periclymenum* '**Belgica**' (**Early Dutch honeysuckle**) No regular pruning is needed, other than occasionally thinning out old and congested shoots after the flowers have faded.

*Lonicera periclymenum* '**Serotina**' (**Late Dutch honeysuckle**) No regular pruning is needed, other than occasionally cutting out old and congested shoots in spring.

The common passion flower (*Passiflora caerulea*) is a spectacular semi-hardy, deciduous Brazilian climber with intricate 7.5cm (3in) wide, white and blue flowers. From early to late summer, trellises are arrayed in flowers.

The Chilean potato tree (*Solanum crispum*) has a bushy, scrambling nature and grows about 4.5m (15ft) high. From early to late summer it reveals 7.5–15cm (3–6in) wide clusters of star-shaped, purple-blue flowers about 2.5cm (1in) wide and with prominent yellow anthers. The form 'Glasnevin' is hardier and more freely flowering.

*Parthenocissus henryana* (**Chinese Virginia creeper** and earlier known as *Vitis henryana*) No regular pruning is needed, other than cutting out dead or overcrowded shoots in spring.

*Parthenocissus quinquefolia* (**true Virginia creeper**) Prune this climber in the same way as for *P. henryana* (*above*).

*Parthenocissus tricuspidata* (**Boston ivy**) Prune this climber in the same way as for *P. henryana* (*above*).

*Passiflora caerulea* (**common passion flower**) In early or mid-spring, cut out tangled shoots to soil level or the main stems. Spur back sideshoots to a growth bud 15cm (6in) from the main stems. *P. umbilicata* can also be grown outdoors in temperate regions.

*Polygonum baldschuanicum* (**Russian vine/Bukhara fleece flower**) Usually, no pruning is needed, but trim back large and invasive climbers in spring.

*Schizophragma integrifolium* and *S. hydrangeoides* Cut out dead flowers and unwanted shoots from wall-trained plants in autumn. Those plants which are climbing into trees can be left alone.

*Solanum crispum* (**Chilean potato tree**) The only pruning that is necessary is to trim back the previous season's growth in mid-spring to 15cm (6in) long. Also, cut out any weak shoots, and those that have been killed by frost.

*Solanum jasminoides* (**jasmine nightshade**) In spring, thin out weak shoots and cut out those damaged by frost.

LEFT *Schizophragma integrifolia* is an ideal climber for covering a pergola, wall or tree trunk, where it attaches itself by aerial roots. It often grows 6m (20ft) high and from mid-summer to autumn displays 30cm (12in) wide clusters of small white flowers surrounded by white bracts, each up to 8cm (3½in) long. *S. hydrangeoides* has creamy-white flowers and pale yellow bracts.

ABOVE Japanese Crimson Glory Vine (*Vitis coignetiae*) is a vigorous deciduous climber with tendrils that are ideal for covering large walls, fences and old tree stumps. The mid-green leaves with heart-shaped bases and three or five pointed lobes are often 30cm (12in) wide and turn brilliant scarlet and crimson in autumn. Some specimens have been known to grow 25m (80ft) high, clinging to old buildings and climbing into large trees.

Native to Japan, this plant was first described in European journals in 1887. The plants had been raised from seeds collected in 1875 by Mme Coignet, who was travelling with her husband.

*Trachelospermum jasminoides* (**star jasmine/confederate jasmine**) During early and mid-spring, thin out vigorous shoots to restrict excessively rampant plants.

*Vitis coignetiae* (**Japanese crimson glory vine**) No regular pruning is needed, except to attempt to restrict growth by cutting out old shoots in late summer. At the same time, shorten young growths.

*Wisteria floribunda* (**Japanese wisteria**) See page 39.

*Wisteria sinensis* (**Chinese wisteria**) Prune in the same way as for *W. floribunda*, see page 39.

Wisterias are perhaps the most spectacular and best-known flowering climbers for covering walls and pergolas or even climbing into trees. During late spring and early summer, this deciduous climber becomes covered in pendulous clusters of fragrant blue or white pea-shaped flowers.

# PRUNING CLEMATIS

The pruning instructions recommended for clematis are often complicated and confusing. This need not be so, for these popular climbers can be separated into just three groups, according to the age of each plant's shoots when they bear flowers.

The first group contains species and hybrids that flower in summer and autumn on shoots produced during the same season. Clematis in this group begin new growth in spring each year by developing fresh, young shoots from the ends of old shoots. Therefore, if left unpruned the bases of plants soon become bare and unsightly.

The second group is formed of vigorous spring- and early summer-flowering types that bear flowers on short shoots which arise from growths that developed during the previous year.

The third group encompasses the hybrids which bear flowers from late spring to mid-summer on shoots produced during the previous year. This means that during any one year, as well as flowering on the previous year's growths, the plant is also producing shoots that will bear flowers later in the same year, creating a second and welcome flush of colour during late summer and into early autumn.

## LARGE-FLOWERED HYBRIDS

Some clematis catalogues classify these superb hybrids into six groups. However, to simplify their pruning, they can be arranged into two main types. For example, Jackmanii, Texensis and Viticella types can be pruned in the way suggested here for Group One, while Florida, Lanuginosa and Patens types may be pruned as recommended for Group Three (SEE PAGE 47).

**Group One** includes:
- *C. jackmanii* hybrids – such as 'Comtesse de Bouchaud', 'Hagley Hybrid' and 'Mrs Cholmondeley'
- *C. orientalis*
- *C. tangutica*
- *C. texensis* hybrids – including 'Etoile Rose' and 'Gravetye Beauty'
- *C. viticella* hybrids – including 'Ernest Markham', 'Lady Betty Balfour' and 'Ville de Lyon'

'Comtesse de Bouchard'

**Pruning Group One**

*1* During late winter after planting, cut back the main shoot to the lowest pair of strong buds. Rigorously cutting back the plant in this way encourages the development of fresh shoots. During the following summer, healthy young shoots develop and must be trained and secured against a wire or wooden framework. Pruning a clematis vigorously in this way encourages the development of strong shoots from ground level, creating a bushy plant.

*2* In late winter of the second year, cut back each shoot to its lowest pair of strong buds. This also includes shoots that developed from ground level during the previous year and are starting to form a bushy plant. During the following summer, vigorous shoots develop and, again, they must be spaced out and secured to a supporting framework. From mid- to late summer flowers will appear on shoots produced earlier in the same season.

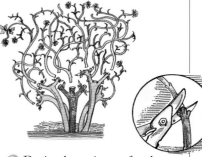

*3* During late winter of each subsequent year, cut all growths back to leave a pair of strong buds at their base. In the same way as in the previous years, shoots grow from these buds and bear flowers from mid-summer to autumn. Tie shoots to a framework. If a plant becomes neglected, cut half of the stems back into older wood to encourage the development of shoots from ground level; cut the others back to buds. The following year, cut back the other half.

**Group Two** includes:
* *C. alpina* – including 'Frances Rivis'
* *C. armandii* – including 'Apple Blossom' and 'Snowdrift'
* *C. chrysocoma*
* *C. macropetala* – including 'Markham's Pink'
* *C. montana* – as well as its many forms such as 'Alexander', 'Elizabeth', 'Rubens' and 'Tetrarose'

ABOVE *Clematis montana*

**Group Three** includes:
* Lanuginosa types – including 'Beauty of Worcester', 'Nelly Moser', 'W. E. Gladstone' and 'William Kennett'
* Patens types – including 'Barbara Dibley', 'Lasurstern', 'Marcel Moser', 'Marie Boisselot', 'The President' and 'Vyvyan Pennell'

ABOVE 'Marie Boisselot'

**Pruning Group Two**

 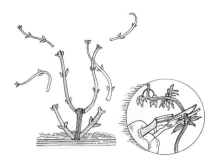 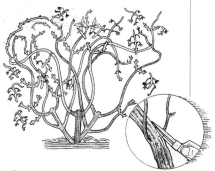

*1* During late winter of the first year after being planted, prune plants by cutting the stem to slightly above the lowest pair of healthy, strong buds. This severe pruning encourages the development of strong shoots that will help to form the climber's framework. During the summer space out and secure these stems to a permanent framework of wires or a wooden trellis. The initial training of shoots is important to ensure that light and air are able to reach the shoots.

*2* In the late winter of the second year, cut back by half the lengths of the main shoots that developed during the previous year and were secured to a supporting framework. Ensure each shoot is cut back to slightly above a pair of strong, healthy buds. If shoots low down on the climber develop flowers early in the year, cut them back to one pair of buds from their base. During the summer, fresh shoots will grow – space them out and secure to the supporting framework.

*3* During early summer of the following and subsequent years, use secateurs to cut back all growths that produced flowers earlier in the year to one or two buds from their point of origin. Within this group, the mountain clematis (*C. montana*) and *C. chrysocoma* are very vigorous and sometimes left unpruned. This eventually creates a tangled plant: rejuvenate by cutting to near ground level in late winter. When these two clematis are allowed to scale trees, leave them unpruned.

**Pruning Group Three**

 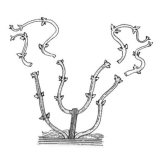 

*1* During late winter after being planted, cut back the stem to the lowest pair of strong, healthy buds. During late spring and early summer, young shoots will grow rapidly and need to be trained and secured to a framework of wires or a wooden trellis. Shoots will also develop from ground level and these, too, should be trained to the framework. Occasionally, a few flowers are produced during the first year.

*2* In late winter of the second year, cut back by half all the main shoots which were produced during the previous year. Sever them just above a pair of strong, healthy buds. During the following summer, train the new shoots and space them out on the supporting framework. In this second season, plants usually develop a few flowers on new growth, often into autumn. Creating a strong framework of shoots is essential.

*3* During early and mid-summer of the third and subsequent years, immediately after the first flush of flowers have faded, cut out a quarter to a third of mature shoots to within 30cm (12in) of the plant's base. When plants are grown against a wall, the shoots can be readily reached and the above pruning is ideal. However, when grown on a pergola, stems cannot be untangled and plants are therefore best left unpruned.

# HEDGES AND TOPIARY

Hedges have both a functional and an aesthetic role in a garden; in the Middle Ages they were solely used to keep out wandering animals and people, while miniature box hedges were later used to create neat, raised edges to borders. Today many hedges planted along the perimeters of gardens still have a defensive nature, especially when clipped to form crenellations, but there are also informal hedges, some abounding in flowers, others with attractive leaves. Internal hedges, perhaps to separate one part of a garden from another or just as a decorative feature alongside a path, are also popular. Lavender forms an attractive – and scented – internal hedge. Whatever the nature and purpose of a hedge, its early pruning while being established, as well as regular attention later, is essential.

Topiary, the art of shaping shrubs, trees and evergreen conifers, has been known for about two thousand years, although there have been periods when it was not popular in fashionable circles. Nevertheless, it persisted in cottage gardens and has became a popular art form.

## FOLIAGE HEDGES

Evergreen shrubs and conifers with attractive foliage are still the most popular plants used to form hedges, although increasingly flowering shrubs are being employed. Part of this change of allegiance from the use of privet (*Ligustrum ovalifolium*) has been the trend away from 'boxed-off' front gardens to open-plan designs. If a defensive or view-blocking hedge is not needed, a front garden with a width of 9m (30ft) can save up to 8.5sq m (90sq ft) of space. This is because a privet hedge, when overgrown, could easily form a barrier 90cm (3ft) thick. Such hedges also impoverish soil around them. Nevertheless, alongside roads and in cold, wind-exposed areas they are invaluable for deadening noise and giving protection against wind. In exposed areas, evergreen hedges are frequently the first features to be established in gardens.

OPPOSITE **Yew** *(Taxus baccata)* forms a superb evergreen hedge and can be used to highlight other plants and sculptured figures. Like *Buxus sempervirens* (above) it can also be used to create topiary.

## FLOWERING HEDGES

There are flowering hedges for boundaries as well as decorative internal ones. For many years the common hawthorn (*Crataegus monogyna*) was used to create hedges in rural areas, where its thorns prevented the entry of animals and its white, heavily scented flowers formed a welcome display in late spring and early summer. It still has its uses, but in urban gardens the evergreen and winter-flowering laurustinus (*Viburnum tinus*) has more charm and forms an attractive feature from late autumn to late spring or early summer.

In countries with a Mediterranean climate, *Hibiscus rosa-sinensis* forms a spectacular hedge. Colourful flowers are also possible in temperate regions, with escallonias, lavender, shrubby potentilla, rhododendrons, roses and rosemary creating bright, highly scented screens.

# PRUNING AND CLIPPING HEDGES

Hedges are often the most neglected plants in a garden. In fact, they need as much attention during their infancy as other plants, and continued clipping and training during their adult life. The range of hedges is wide, but basically those with a formal outline are usually grown for their foliage, and informal types with irregular shapes are planted for their beautiful leaves or flowers. Many of the most popular hedging plants are featured on pages 54 to 59, with details of their initial and subsequent pruning.

Some of these hedging and screening plants are evergreen conifers; others are shrubs and either deciduous or evergreen. For many years during the middle part of this century, the all-green privet or the golden-leaved type were mainly used to form hedges. Although they still have a role in gardens, there are many other hedging plants to consider.

## FORMAL HEDGES

Formal hedges usually have a clean, crisp outline and are invariably formed of evergreen conifers, small-leaved evergreen shrubs and deciduous shrubs. These latter ones include beech (*Fagus sylvatica*), hornbeam (*Carpinus betulus*) and hawthorn (*Crataegus monogyna*). The beech forms a moderately high, thick hedge, with superb coloured leaves in autumn. Even when their colours fade, the leaves remain on the hedge for several months. The eventual size of beech often prevents its wider use, especially for elderly gardeners who are unable to climb ladders and, with safety, use electrical hedge clippers.

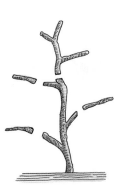

*1* Deciduous, formal hedging plants must be cut down by about half and have all sideshoots cut back by a similar amount immediately after being planted. When bought as bare-rooted plants, planting is from late autumn to early spring. For container-grown plants, plant at any time when the soil is workable.

*2* During the following year, from late autumn to early spring, again severely cut back the leading shoot and sideshoots, by about a half. This may appear to be too drastic and to lose much of the plant, but unless pruning is severe the base of the hedge will be unsightly and bare of stems and leaves in summer.

*3* In the third winter, cut back all new shoots by a third. During the following season, shoots which develop will be bushy and start to form a solid screen of leaves. During a hedge's infancy, water it regularly and feed it in spring and mid-summer to encourage the development of fresh young shoots.

---

### SHAPING A HEDGE

**Creating a uniform shape along a hedge's entire length is essential. To establish a uniform height, a taut string stretched between stout poles is ideal over a short distance, but a better way is to use a template. For the shape to choose in areas of heavy snowfalls see page 51.**

Round top          Flat top

## CONIFEROUS HEDGES

Evergreen coniferous hedges, such as the Leyland cypress (× *Cupressocyparis leylandii*), Lawson's cypress (*Chamaecyparis lawsoniana*) and western red cedar (*Thuja plicata*), form superb hedges. Some, such as the Leyland cypress, are too large for most gardens, while others are smaller and create screens of attractive and colourful foliage throughout the year.

When the leading shoots reach 15–30cm (6-12in) above the desired height, cut off their tops about 15cm (6in) below this point. This then leaves sufficient space for the hedge's top to create a bushy nature which is at the desired height of the hedge.

ABOVE Large-leaved evergreen shrubs must be pruned with sharp secateurs rather than hand shears that can chop leaves in half and create an unsightly mess. Always cut shoots back to just above a leaf-joint. Later, fresh shoots will develop and hide the cuts. Do not position the cut so that a short piece of stem is left. This is unsightly and may cause the onset of decay. Some large-leaved evergreen hedges are formed of plants grown solely for their attractive leaves, such as the popular and widely grown variegated laurel (*Aucuba japonica* 'Variegata'), while others like laurustinus (*Viburnum tinus*) are better known for their flowers.

## RENOVATING OLD HEDGES

Hedges in old gardens often become neglected, too large and bare of shoots and stems at their bases. They encroach on neighbouring plants and impoverish the soil, as well as obscuring the light and becoming full of old, dusty leaves and stems. However, it is frequently possible to renovate some of them.

❋ If the hedge is too wide it can be cut back in spring, but often this is too drastic all at once and is better spread over two or three seasons. In the first year, cut back the top to the desired height, and in the second year prune either one or both of the sides. Not all hedging plants can be severely cut back, but those that can include spotted laurel (*Aucuba japonica* 'Variegata'), beech (*Fagus sylvatica*), box (*Buxus sempervirens*), elaeagnus, forsythia, gorse (*Ulex europaeus*), hawthorn (*Crataegus monogyna*), privet (*Ligustrum ovalifolium*), firethorn (*Pyracantha*), rhododendrons and yew (*Taxus baccata*).

❋ Rosemary (*Rosmarinus officinalis*) and lavender (*Lavandula spica*) often become tall and straggly, especially when not trimmed annually. Rather than cutting them back severely, they are best replaced with young plants. Replace some of the soil if the hedge is to be in the same position.

❋ Overgrown conifers, with the exception of yew (*Taxus baccata*), should not be drastically cut back as this radically spoils them. However, the tops of conifers can be cut out from young hedges when the desired height has been reached (*see above left*).

### SNOWFALL SHAPES

Rain cleanses hedges of dust and dirt, but heavy snowfalls often cause irreparable damage to them, the weight breaking and splaying shoots outwards. Instead of a square top, choose a rounded or sloped outline, so that snow has a better chance to fall off. In warm areas, where there is little risk of snow, the top of a hedge can be cut with more of a square outline.

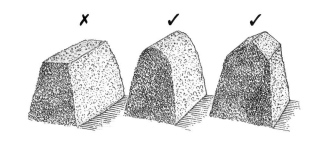

ABOVE Small-leaved hedging such as privet is traditionally trimmed using hand shears. Modern hand shears are lighter to use than earlier ones and do not judder wrists and hands so violently. Nevertheless, for many gardeners they are still difficult to use, especially on a large hedge. There are electrically-powered types: some cut on both sides of the blades, others only on one. Where distance from a power supply is great, rechargeable types can be used (see page 6 for electrical safety). Use ear-muffs to reduce the risk of damage to ears (below).

## EVERGREEN HEDGES

The most popular of the small-leaved evergreen shrubs used as hedges are privet (*Ligustrum ovalifolium*), its golden-leaved form, and the shrubby honeysuckle (*Lonicera nitida*), together with its golden-leaved variety 'Baggesen's Gold'. When planted, these must be treated in the same way as for the deciduous types on the opposite page.

Large-leaved evergreen shrubs, which invariably create informal hedges, need little initial pruning other than cutting back long shoots to just above a leaf-joint. However, cutting back the tips to slightly above leaves encourages bushiness and the development of stronger shoots. At the same time, cut out disease or pest-damaged shoots.

If, during the second season, large-leaved shrubs are not creating a bushy outline, cut a few shoots back to encourage the development of sideshoots.

# PRUNING AND TRAINING TECHNIQUES FOR TOPIARY

There is a certain romance about topiary, whether seen in a classical setting depicting various geometric shapes or in a cottage garden where a peacock has been created out of the small-leaved box or shrubby honeysuckle (*Lonicera nitida*). Topiary does not have to be on the grand scale to be fun: a small sphere is just as satisfying for a novice as a more ambitious animal shape for an experienced enthusiast. In earlier times, large-leaved evergreens, such as laurel, were used, but this created features too large for cottage and other small gardens. Also, laurel is difficult to clip without damaging the leaves.

Evergreen shrubs are the plants mainly used to form topiary, but deciduous shrubs such as forsythia, crab apples and laburnums are sometimes employed. Indeed, a standard forsythia in spring is unforgettable, but does not have the year-round attraction of evergreens, especially those fashioned in the image of birds and animals.

## CREATING A SIMPLE DESIGN

**A cone formed by a conifer such as yew or arbor-vitae is an ideal subject for beginners. Use only one plant, tie it to a support and when a shoot reaches about 15cm (6in) above the top, cut it off. Trim it to shape regularly.**

**PLANTS TO CONSIDER**
Small-leaved evergreens which can be used to form topiary subjects include:
• Arbor-vitae (*Thuja occidentalis* – and varieties): Evergreen conifers, ideal for simple topiary sculptures and suitable for growing in containers. It forms topiary subjects up to 1.5m (5ft) high.
• Box *(Buxus sempervirens)*: Slow-growing, with small, aromatic, glossy-green leaves. It is ideal for forming birds and animals as well as geometric shapes up to 1.2m (4ft) high. It grows very well in containers. There are several varieties with variegated leaves.

Simple cone-shapes are easily formed and maintained. They look superb when displayed in pairs.

Birds and other animals are made more distinctive by creating them on a plinth.

Spirals or corkscrews are easier to train and shape than might be thought.

* Privet (*Ligustrum ovalifolium*): Shiny, green leaves, but can be semi-evergreen in cold regions. The leaves are larger than those of the shrubby honeysuckle. There is a golden-leaved form. Privet is not suitable for planting in containers.

* Shrubby honeysuckle (*Lonicera nitida*): Prolific grower with small, shiny, dark-green leaves clustered around stiff stems. It is ideal for subjects up to 75cm (2½ft) high and long. The form 'Baggesen's Gold' has golden leaves. Both forms can be grown in tubs.

* Yew (*Taxus baccata*): Small-leaved evergreen conifer bearing dark-green leaves. It forms topiary subjects up to 2.4m (8ft) high. It will grow in containers.

**Keep it simple**

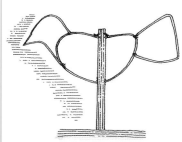
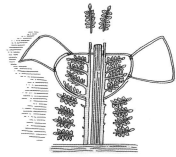
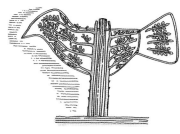

*1* Never be too ambitious when embarking on topiary; an identifiable sphere, cone or small bird is better than a deformed kangaroo! Although topiary experts are often able to create simple forms without the aid of a wire outline, for novices they are essential and they are best put in place before setting the plants in position. Secure the framework – not longer than 90cm (3ft) – to a strong stake.

*2* Plant two topiary subjects on each side of the wooden stake. Loosely tie them to the stake and train them upwards until their tops are about 23cm (9in) above the framework. Then, preferably in spring, cut them level with the top of the framework. Also, cut off the lower shoots close to the stem. Select three or four shoots on each plant; first grow them vertically, shorten by a third and then train horizontally.

*3* When the horizontal shoots have grown about 15cm (6in) past the main body, cut them back. Cutting the stems back radically each time ensures the development of stronger shoots more than if just their tips were removed. Do not be in a hurry for shoots to reach the ends of the framework: it is much more important to build up a strong internal body of shoots that are firm and mature.

BELOW  Tiered spheres are easy to train and more interesting than when displayed as a single ball-like feature.

RIGHT  This topiary bird can be formed singularly or as one of an interesting and eye-catching group.

The handles on jugs or urns are more complex to form and maintain.

# HEDGING PLANTS

Many shrubs and conifers can be encouraged to form hedges, either as a boundary alongside a road or to divide one part of a garden from another – or even as a decorative feature such as in a knot garden, where dwarf hedges line paths and beds of herbs or flowers. Evergreen, semi-evergreen and deciduous plants can all be used. In addition to shrubs and conifers, wonderful screens can be made from bamboos. Eventually they form dense thickets without the need for any pruning, except as a remedial treatment should they become damaged. *Arundinaria japonica*, for instance, grows up to 4.5m (15ft) high, with dark, glossy-green leaves. *A. nitida* is less vigorous and has purple stems and bright-green leaves (*see page 20*). For a lower hedge, *Sasa veitchii* is better, forming a dense thicket up to 1.2m (4ft) high. The large, green leaves have light, straw-coloured edges. The only pruning necessary with bamboos is to cut out damaged stems after heavy falls of snow which has been allowed to remain on top of them for several days.

*Aucuba japonica* **'Variegata' (spotted laurel)** Pruning is not usually necessary, but use sharp and strong secateurs to cut back old stems in spring.

*Berberis darwinii* **(Darwin's berberis)** In early summer, after the flowers have faded, use secateurs to cut back long stems to create an overall even shape and thickness.

*Berberis × stenophylla* Prune this hybrid in the same way as for *B. darwinii*.

*Berberis thunbergii* **(Japanese berberis)** Trim to shape with secateurs in winter, but wait until the berries have dropped.

*Berberis thunbergii* **'Atropurpurea Nana'** Trim to shape with secateurs in winter.

*Buxus sempervirens* **'Suffruticosa' (edging box)** Trim to shape with hand shears in late summer or wait until early autumn.

*Carpinus betulus* **(common hornbeam/European hornbeam)** Use hand shears to clip hedges to shape during mid-summer.

*Chamaecyparis lawsoniana* **(Lawson's cypress)** Widely used for hedging; many varieties. Once established, use hand shears or powered clippers as necessary.

When attempting to limit the height, cut off the top about 15cm (6in) below the desired point. This then enables sideshoots to form an attractive top at the desired height. If plants are allowed to grow 60cm (2ft) or more above the desired height before they are cut back it will result in a sparse top that, if seen from above, looks hideous. Therefore, always limit the height of conifers while they are still small and soon able to reclothe their tops.

*Cupressus macrocarpa* 'Goldcrest', an evergreen conifer, forms a tall hedge with feathery, rich-yellow foliage.

*Berberis* × *stenophylla*, a vigorous, evergreen shrub, has arching stems with narrow, deep-green leaves and golden-yellow flowers during spring and early summer. It forms a large hedge, often 1.8m (6ft) high and 1.5m (5ft) wide, and is ideal in a semi-formal or informal setting. Although long stems can be pruned after the flowers fade, it never has a formal outline.

Edging box (*Buxus sempervirens* 'Suffruticosa') forms neat, dwarf, evergreen hedges up to 23–30cm (9–12in) high and 20–25cm (8–10in) wide. The glossy, rounded, green leaves form a superb edging alongside paths. Alternatively, they can be used to create knot gardens.

ABOVE The yellow-leaved form of Leyland cypress (x *Cupressocyparis leylandii* 'Castlewellan') is less vigorous than the all-green form, which is better used to create a tall and thick windbreak.

***Cotoneaster lacteus*** Use secateurs to cut off long shoots after the flowers have faded. At the same time, cut back the current season's shoots to where berries are forming.

***Cotoneaster simonsii*** A semi-evergreen, with an erect habit and ideal for forming hedges. Use secateurs to trim hedges during late winter or early spring. Trim deciduous cotoneasters in late summer or early autumn.

***Crataegus monogyna* (common hawthorn/quick/May)** Use hand shears to trim hedges to shape at any time after the flowers have faded and until late winter. Where hedges have become neglected, cut them back in late summer – they will soon break into growth during the following year, even after having been cut severely.

**× *Cupressocyparis leylandii* (Leyland cypress)** Use garden shears to clip to shape in late summer or early autumn. When attempting to limit the height, cut off the top about 15cm (6in) below the desired point. This then enables sideshoots to form and an attractive top at the desired height to be formed.

**× *Cupressocyparis leylandii* 'Castlewellan'** Prune in the same way as for × *C. leylandii*.

***Cupressus macrocarpa* 'Goldcrest'** Use hand shears to trim this hedge during its early years. Afterwards, little trimming is needed. When limiting its height, cut off the top about 15cm (6in) below the desired point. This then enables sideshoots to form and an attractive top to be created at the height that is required.

LEFT *Ilex* × *altaclarensis* 'Golden Queen' is a hardy, evergreen shrub that creates a hedge up to 3m (10ft) high and 1.2m (4ft) wide. The thick, leathery, dark-green, shiny leaves have golden edges.

*Escallonia* 'Donard Seedling' is a slightly tender evergreen shrub, ideal for forming a hedge in a mild climate. The long, arching branches bear apple-blossom-pink flowers during early and mid-summer.

*Escallonia* Once the hedge is established, shoots can be cut back hard after the flowers have faded. A more abundantly flowered hedge can be created by only trimming stems lightly.

*Euonymus japonicus* (**spindle tree**) A slightly tender evergreen shrub. Use secateurs to clip it to shape in mid-spring. If a formal outline is desired, trim with hand shears during summer.

*Fagus sylvatica* (**common beech**) Newly planted hedges must be immediately cut back by a half to a quarter to encourage the development of shoots from each plant's base. Once established, use hand shears or powered clippers to trim it to shape in mid- or late summer.

*Griselinia littoralis* Use secateurs to trim back hedges in early or mid-summer.

*Griselinia littoralis* '**Dixon's Cream**' Prune in the same way as for *G. littoralis (above)*, but not quite so severely.

*Hippophae rhamnoides* (**sea buckthorn**) During late summer, use secateurs to cut back long, straggly shoots.

*Ilex* × *altaclerensis* Use secateurs to trim hedges in mid-spring. Cut neglected holly hedges back in spring.

*Ilex aquifolium* (**common holly/English holly**) Prune in the same way as for *I.* × *altaclerensis* (*above*).

*Lavandula spica,* often sold as *L. angustifolia* or *L. officinalis* (**lavender/old English lavender**) Pinch out newly planted hedges to encourage sideshoots. Use garden shears to clip established hedges to shape in early or mid-spring. Prune straggly plants back quite heavily.

*Ligustrum ovalifolium* (**common privet**) Once the hedge is established, use hand shears to clip over it several times during summer.

*Ligustrum ovalifolium* '**Aureo-marginatum**', also known as *L. o.* 'Aureum' (**golden privet**) It is slightly less vigorous than the all-green type and therefore needs harder pruning during its formative years. However,

Griselinia littoralis 'Variegata' forms an evergreen shrub, bearing shiny green leaves with white variegations. 'Dixon's Cream' is another variegated form, with leaves splashed and mottled creamy-white. It is an ideal shrub for planting in warm coastal areas.

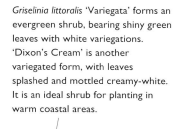

LEFT  The golden privet (Ligustrum ovalifolium 'Aureo-marginatum' but also known as L. o. 'Aureum') is slightly less vigorous than the all-green species and is evergreen in all but the coldest winters. The glossy leaves are often completely yellow, although sometimes they have green centres. Where hedges are a mixture of green and yellow privet, use two yellow plants to one of green.

Potentilla fruticosa 'Katherine Dykes' forms a dome-shaped deciduous shrub about 1.5m (5ft) high and wide. Throughout most of summer it is smothered in large, buttercup-like, primrose-yellow flowers, about 2.5cm (1in) across.

once established it needs regular clipping in the same way as the all-green type.

***Lonicera nitida* (Chinese honeysuckle)** Cut back newly planted hedges by a half and in the next year clip the young growths several times. During the following few years, cut back new growths by a half.

***Olearia × haastii* (daisy bush)** Use secateurs to cut out dead shoots in mid-spring, at the same time cutting back long shoots to create an interesting, informal outline.

***Pittosporum tenuifolium***
Use garden shears to trim established hedges in mid-spring and early to mid-summer.

***Potentilla fruticosa* (shrubby cinquefoil)** Use secateurs to cut back the tips of shoots when the flowers have faded. Also cut out weak and old shoots at their bases to encourage the development of further stems.

RIGHT  Olearia ilicifolia (Maori holly) is an evergreen shrub 2.4–3m (8–10ft) high and wide. During early summer it develops small, daisy-like flowers with a musky fragrance. These are borne amid narrow, leathery, holly-like leaves. Prune this in the same way as Olearia haastii (detailed above).

**_Prunus_ × _cistena_ 'Crimson Dwarf'** **(purple-leaf sand cherry)** Use secateurs to trim to shape after the flowers have faded in late spring.

**_Prunus laurocerasus_ (cherry laurel/common laurel)** Use secateurs to trim back shoots in late spring or late summer. Where hedges have grown too large, cut them hard back during spring.

**_Prunus lusitanica_ (Portugal laurel)** Prune in the same way as for _P. laurocerasus_ (_above_).

**_Pyracantha rogersiana_ (firethorn)** When planted, use secateurs to cut plants back by half, and during the following summer pinch back young shoots by about 15cm (6in). Repeat this during the following year. When established, use secateurs to trim plants during early summer, but the farther back a plant is cut, the fewer berries it will subsequently bear.

**_Rhododendron luteum_** No regular pruning is needed, other than cutting out dead or crossing branches after the flowers have faded.

**_Rosmarinus officinalis_ 'Miss Jessop's Upright'** Use secateurs to cut out dead shoots in early spring. Also cut out straggly and misplaced shoots. Where plants have become overgrown, cut back all shoots by half in mid-spring.

**_Symphoricarpos albus_ 'White Hedge' (snowberry)** Thin out overgrown hedges in winter. Use secateurs to trim established hedges to shape several times during summer.

**_Tamarix pentandra_ (tamarisk)** It is ideal as a windbreak or hedging plant in coastal

RIGHT _Pyracantha rogersiana_, a Firethorn, has narrow, mid-green leaves and clusters of white flowers in early summer, followed by bright, orange-red berries during autumn and into winter. The form 'Flava' has exceptionally attractive bright yellow berries.

gardens in mild areas. To produce hedges that are bushy at their bases, cut newly planted plants to 30cm (12in) high. Later, use secateurs to cut out the tips of the sideshoots when 15cm (6in) long. Once established, use secateurs in late winter or early spring to cut back the previous season's shoots to within 15cm (6in) of the points from where they originated. Because tamarisk is usually only grown as a hedge in warm coastal areas, it can be pruned earlier than when grown inland as a specimen feature.

**_Taxus baccata_ (common yew/English yew)** Start off with small plants and when 30cm (12in) high, nip out the growing tips to encourage bushiness. This will be necessary several times during the early years. Later, clip with hand shears in late summer.

_Rhododendron luteum_ (also known as _Azalea luteum_) is a deciduous shrub that creates a magnificent display of fragrant, yellow flowers during late spring and early summer. In autumn the matt-green leaves assume shades of rich scarlet. Although it is often grown as a specimen shrub in a wild garden, it is even better when planted as a background hedge. Acid soil is essential. Although widely grown and seen by some gardeners as 'ordinary', it nevertheless seldom fails to create an attractive feature.

Rosemary (*Rosmarinus officinalis*) mainly flowers during late spring and early summer, but often continues to bloom sporadically until autumn. It forms a superb evergreen shrub, with aromatic, dark-green leaves and mauve flowers. The form 'Miss Jessop's Upright' is more vigorous and taller, with light-blue flowers.

ABOVE *Thujya plicata* (western red cedar) forms a formal hedge that can be clipped to form arches. The pineapple-scented leaves are shiny and mid-green.

***Thuya occidentalis* (white cedar,** sometimes known as *Thuja*) Use hand shears to trim in late summer. When limiting its height, cut off the top about 15cm (6in) below the desired point. This then enables sideshoots to form and an attractive top to be created at the desired height.

***Thuya plicata* (western red cedar,** sometimes known as *Thuja)* Prune in the same way as for *T. occidentalis* (*above*).

***Viburnum tinus* (laurustinus)** No regular pruning is needed, other than using secateurs to cut out dead and misplaced shoots when the flowers have faded in spring.

The common yew (*Taxus baccata*) has been used for centuries to create evergreen hedges. The massed, narrow, dark-green leaves create a superb foil and wind-sheltered area for other garden plants, especially those with a herbaceous nature.

# ROSES

Roses are part of our gardening heritage and, although native only to the northern hemisphere, they are now grown throughout the world. The range of types and varieties of roses is wide, partly a result of the natural promiscuity of many wild roses but also because of our involvement with them.

Like many other woody, long-lived garden plants, roses are also shrubs and to encourage an annual feast of flowers regular pruning is essential. It not only creates magnificent flowers, but ensures the shrub's longevity, especially when it has been planted in poor soil. The quality and size of flowers can also be influenced by the severity with which plants are pruned. The type of pruning needed by Hybrid Tea roses (now known as Large-flowered roses) is quite different from that required by a rambler rose or those used to form hedges.

Regrettably, there has developed a mystique about pruning roses that has deterred many gardeners from growing them, and yet these floriferous shrubs are some of the most tolerant of all garden shrubs to bad pruning. If a Hybrid Tea rose is too severely pruned, only a few stems will develop but they will bear large blooms. Conversely, if lightly pruned many but smaller flowers are produced.

### VARIED NATURES

Some roses form bushes, others hug the ground, while a few scale trees or obligingly lean against walls, pergolas or trellises. And, by inserting buds at the tops of tall rootstocks, standard roses can be created. Some roses flower directly on shoots produced from the plant's base, while others develop flowers on young shoots that originate from an existing framework. Each of these roses needs different treatment to encourage the regular creation of flowers.

### RESILIENT ROSES

Pruning bush forms of Hybrid Teas (Large-flowered roses) and Floribundas (Cluster-flowered roses) has, for many rose lovers, acquired a cult status that has caused unnecessary concern among

ABOVE To many gardeners, roses are the epitome of a colourful and scented garden. LEFT 'Félicité et Perpétue' is a superb climber, that bears clusters of small, creamy-white flowers in early to mid-summer.

novice rose growers. Within this book we have presented the traditional methods of pruning, but it is necessary to remember that trials during recent years have involved pruning bush roses with garden shears, just clipping over them. Subsequent flowering has been good, but the long-term effects on the bushes are unknown. Nevertheless, it does substantiate the claim that roses are more resilient and undemanding than many rose growers believed.

Even expert rose pruners differ in their pruning recommendations: for standard roses, for example, some experts suggest the method detailed on pages 64 and 65, while others advocate using garden shears and clipping them back by a third to a half, and every fourth year pruning out some old and twiggy wood.

# PRUNING BUSH ROSES

Pruning Hybrid Tea roses (Large-flowered roses) and Floribunda roses (Cluster-flowered roses) has acquired an unnecessary mystique, yet basically it is very logical, and entirely influenced by the nature of these plants. Both types of roses are deciduous shrubs that produce their best flowers on new shoots developed earlier in the year. The size and number of new shoots that bush roses develop each year is dictated by the degree of severity with which they are pruned. Pruning is also influenced by the type of soil, whether exhibition blooms are desired and if the plants are young. This may appear complicated, but if taken stage by stage becomes quite straightforward. Usually, after a couple of years of pruning bush roses, it becomes clear what degree of severity is required for garden roses.

**MAKING THE RIGHT CUT**
Part of the technique of pruning roses is to make clean cuts slightly above outward-pointing buds. This is achieved by using sharp secateurs that are large enough to tackle the work. Never use small secateurs as they become strained and produce torn, ragged surfaces that do not heal quickly. Pages 6 and 7 detail the types of pruning tool available. Choose one that will achieve cuts with clean, smooth surfaces.

If you are left-handed, remember that some secateurs have been specially designed for you and enable cuts to be made much more easily than with right-handed types. They also enable left-handed gardeners to see the position of each cut more easily than if using a right-handed pair.

Cuts more than 12mm (½ in) wide should be painted with a fungicidal wound-paint to prevent the entry of diseases, and to give protection from dampness and frost.

**TAKE CARE NOT TO MAKE THESE CUTS**

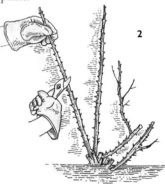

Too far above the bud, causing the shoot to die (left).
Result of using blunt or too small secateurs (centre).
Too close to the bud, leaving it partly unsupported (right).

**PREPARATORY PRUNING**
Whether pruning Hybrid Tea or Floribunda bush roses, the initial task is the same.

*1* Cut out dead wood directly at the shrub's base. Also, remove shoots that have been damaged by wind blowing them against each other, and cut out those infected by diseases. If the cut surface is brown, the stem is infected and a lower cut is needed where the wood is white. Always ensure that damaged shoots are not left on a plant.

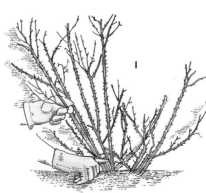

2

*2* Cut out thin, weak and spindly shoots, right to their bases. Ensure that the centre of the shrub is open and that air can circulate throughout the bush. This helps shoots to ripen, enabling them to resist the entry of disease spores.

## THE CORRECT CUT

**All pruning cuts on roses have traditionally been made individually and with sharp secateurs, and although experiments using hedge clippers are now being investigated, for the present it is best to use the well tried and tested method with secateurs.**

Do not leave short stubs at the plant's base: they look unsightly and attract diseases.

Make a slightly sloping cut about 6mm (¼ in) above an outward-pointing, healthy bud.

Use sharp secateurs that are large enough to cut the stem cleanly.

1

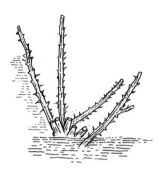

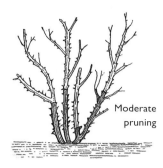

Moderate pruning

**CUT FLOWERS
FOR THE HOME**
Displaying long-stemmed roses indoors is a bonus when growing Hybrid Tea types. A flower develops to its maximum size when the small buds growing around the central one are removed (disbudding), but pruning also plays a major role. Use the hard or moderate pruning techniques to produce exhibition-standard types, and moderate pruning for flowers to decorate the home.

*3* The shoots that remain should be strong, healthy and spaced out (*above*). The severity of pruning during this last stage is influenced by several factors such as if newly planted, type of soil or whether Hybrid Tea or Floribunda. The next stage is to prune them either 'hard', 'moderately', or 'lightly'.

**Moderate pruning or medium pruning** Stems are cut back by about a half their length, although weak ones need more severe treatment.

Ideal method for most Hybrid Tea and Floribunda roses, especially those growing in ordinary soil. If, after a few years, Hybrid Tea types become too high and leggy, prune hard during one season.

The shape of a flower is more important than its size. Brilliance and freshness is paramount, and each flower must be free from pest and disease damage.

**The severity of pruning**

Hard pruning

Light pruning

Long, straight stem that has not been rubbing or blown against another plant. Ensure plants are fed with a balanced fertilizer; ones mainly containing nitrogen create weak stems.

Large, glossy-surfaced, strongly-green leaves without any blemishes are essential. Damage to them can be caused by pests and diseases, as well as by rubbing against other plants.

**Hard pruning or low pruning**
Stems are cut back to three or four buds above the plant's base. This leaves short stems 13–15cm (5–6in) high.

Ideal for pruning newly planted Hybrid Tea and Floribunda roses, as it encourages strong shoots to develop from the plant's base.

Not a method suited to most established bush roses, although weak-growing Hybrid Teas are frequently hard pruned.

Often used to rejuvenate neglected Hybrid Teas, but not established Floribundas.

**Light pruning or high or long pruning** The top third of all shoots are removed.

Frequently used on vigorous Hybrid Tea roses, as it does not encourage the further growth of strong shoots, and restricts the plant's height.

Ideal method for all bush roses growing in sandy soils, where the fertility is low and insufficient to provide the vigorous growth encouraged by 'hard' pruning.

## WHEN TO PRUNE

**Every rosarian has a particular view about the best time to prune roses, but the consensus is:**

✳ **Established bushes, and autumn- and winter-planted roses, are best pruned in early spring just when growth is starting but before leaves appear.**

✳ **Bushes planted in spring should be pruned immediately after planting.**

✳ **To prevent bushes being buffeted by winds during winter storms, and their roots becoming loosened in the soil, cut back long stems in early winter. If infected with diseases, burn these shoots.**

# PRUNING STANDARD ROSES

Standard roses are especially useful in gardens; they can be planted as centrepieces and focal points as well as dotted among bush types to create height in borders. They are especially useful in formal situations.

Standard roses are usually formed by budding Hybrid Tea (Large-flowered bush) and Floribunda (Cluster-flowered bush) varieties on to the tops of rootstocks that form the strong, upright stems. Full standards have stems 1.2–1.5m (4–5ft) high, half-standards about 90cm (3ft). Half-standards are not as popular as they were in earlier years. Although most standards are formed from Hybrid Tea and Floribunda varieties, some English roses, Old roses and Shrub types also are used (*see page 67*). With all these roses, strong stakes and ties are essential to prevent the stem bending under the weight of flowers and leaves, especially in windy areas or when the foliage is wet and the plants are in full bloom.

### SINGLE OR DOUBLE-BUDDED?

The best and most easily-managed standard roses have two buds inserted into the top of the rootstock. This helps to ensure that from all angles the standard's head is evenly shaped and attractive. It is possible that one bud will grow more vigorously than the other and, if this happens, pruning the weaker shoot more severely than the other one will correct the imbalance.

Where only one bud has been used – and it is best not to buy such a plant – it is essential initially to cut back the shoot that develops from it to three or four eyes so that a strong framework with equally-spaced shoots is created. If this is neglected, the head will never be attractive and evenly balanced. Also, unbalanced heads are more likely to be damaged by strong winds than those with an even spread of shoots.

**Pruning standard roses**

1 During late winter or early spring after being planted, cut back strong stems on Hybrid Tea varieties to three to four eyes of their bases. With Floribundas, cut stems to six to eight eyes.

2 In the following autumn or early winter, cut off the flower heads and completely remove soft, unripe and thin shoots. This reduces the risk of wind damaging the standard's head during early winter.

3 During late winter and early spring of the following year, the first task is to cut out dead, weak and diseased shoots. Also cut out crossing shoots.

4 Cut new shoots on Hybrid Teas to three to five eyes, and laterals to two to four. With Floribundas, cut new shoots to six to eight eyes, and laterals to three to six eyes.

# PRUNING PILLAR ROSES

### ROSES ON POLES

Growing climbing roses on poles 2.4–3m (8–10ft) high is an ideal way to create beacons of colour in gardens, especially if it is not possible to grow them against walls or fences. Suitable varieties have an upright nature, with stems about 3m (10ft) high. Varieties to consider include: 'Aloha' (pink/fragrant), 'Bantry Bay' (rose-pink/slightly fragrant), 'Dortmund' (red, with a white eye), 'Galway Bay' (pink/slightly fragrant), 'Golden Showers' (golden-yellow/fragrant), 'New Dawn' (silvery-pink/scented), 'Pink Perpétué' (rose-pink with a carmine reverse/slightly fragrant) and 'White Cockade' (white/slightly fragrant).

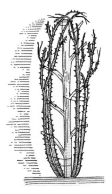

*1* During the first summer after being planted, pillar roses develop long stems. Train these in an upright manner and secure them to a rustic pole, preferably one where a few short branches have been left to create support for stems. They also help to keep the plant's centre open, with a lax appearance.

*2* In the following summer, the plant bears flowers on small, lateral shoots that have grown on the long stems which developed during the previous year. Additionally, during summer, fresh, long shoots develop from the plant's base. Cut off all flowers as they fade to keep the plant tidy – remove the complete flower truss.

*3* During late autumn or early winter of the same year, cut back all lateral shoots which developed flowers. Prune back some of the young shoots produced during the year, attempting to retain a symmetrical outline. Ensure they are spread evenly around the plant and not all clustered on the sunny side.

---

## WEEPING STANDARDS

These are a popular form of standard rose and have a cascading, weeping appearance. They are mainly produced by budding rambler varieties on 1.2–1.8m (4–6ft) tall stems of *Rosa rugosa*. Pruning is quite simple: during late summer or early autumn, completely cut out two-year-old shoots that have flowers. This will leave young shoots that developed earlier during summer to produce flowers in the following year. If there are insufficient young stems to replace the old ones that are cut out, leave a few of these older ones and cut back any lateral shoots on them to two or three eyes. Ensure the main stem is secured to a stake.

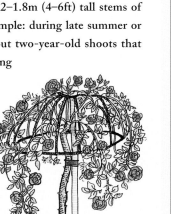

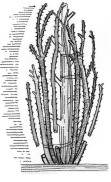

*4* Also in late autumn or early winter of the same year, cut out weak shoots that have developed from the plant's base. Also, remove diseased and dead wood, and totally cut out a few of the very old shoots. The cycle of cutting out old stems and training in new ones must be repeated each year. If this is neglected, the plant will become a mass of tangled shoots that produce very few flowers.

*5* During the following and subsequent years, lateral shoots on the previous year's growth will bear flowers in summer. Cut these off as they fade (*above, left*). In late autumn or early winter of the same year, cut out all laterals that produced flowers. Totally sever old wood and completely remove a few of the old stems (*above, right*). Pillar roses are usually very easy to prune, as all the shoots are easy to reach.

# PRUNING CLIMBERS AND RAMBLERS

Although Climbers and Ramblers have a leaning nature and many happily scale trees or lean against walls, they each have a distinct character. Ramblers develop numerous small flowers that are held in large bunches which appear in early and mid-summer. They flower only once a year and the plant then devotes its energies to producing strong canes which will bear flowers during the following season. Climbers have larger flowers, often similar to other garden roses, and they are borne singly or in small groups. Also, some have the ability to produce further flowers after their first period in bloom. Although these distinctions are clear in theory, they are complicated by the wide range of varieties and varied derivations of both Ramblers and Climbers. The range of Ramblers is detailed below, while Climbers are discussed on the opposite page. Some Climbers – such as 'Golden Showers', 'Pink Perpétue' and 'White Cockade' – are also trained as pillar roses, and these are featured on the previous page.

**RAMBLING ROSES**
There are three main types:
* Multiflora Hybrids: Large bunches of small flowers, with stiff growth. Their pruning is detailed here in Group Two.
* *Sempervirens* Hybrids: Graceful Ramblers, with long, strong growth and sprays of small flowers. Their pruning is described in Group One.

* *Wichuraiana* Hybrids: Long, graceful growths and quite large flowers borne in elegant sprays. They develop long, flexible shoots from their bases. Their pruning is described in Group One, although some rose experts suggest they can be left with little pruning. In such cases, however, they eventually form thickets.

## GROUP TWO

**The pruning of these plants is the same during the first year as for those in Group One (SEE BELOW), which they closely resemble, though they develop fewer shoots from their bases. Prune them immediately after the flowers fade, completely cutting out old shoots and training in new ones. If no basal shoots are present, cut the old stems to within 38cm (15in) of their bases. Also, cut back old shoots higher up on the plant to vigorous sideshoots, and cut short lateral shoots back to two or three eyes above their point of origin.**

**Group One**

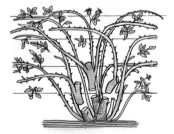
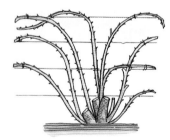

*1* From late autumn to early spring, when a Rambler is received from a nursery, cut back coarse, unevenly long roots. It will also probably have three or four stems, each up to 1.2m (4ft) long. Cut these back to 23–38cm (9–15in) long. Then, plant it firmly in good, well-drained soil.

*2* During spring, young shoots will develop from buds at the top of each stem. These will form the initial flowering stems and framework, although the aim must eventually be to encourage fresh shoots to develop from the plant's base, each and every year.

*3* In late summer or autumn of the following year (as well as all subsequent ones) cut out flowered shoots to their bases, leaving, tying in and spacing out on supports all strong shoots that developed earlier that season. Take care not to damage these shoots by tying them too tightly.

*4* At the same time, cut back all shoots that are growing from these main ones to within two or three eyes of their base. Rejuvenate neglected ramblers by cutting all shoots back. Although this means losing the following season's flowers, it is the best way to restore regular flowering.

## CLIMBING ROSES

There are several types:

• Noisette roses: An old group, with small, rosette-type flowers. They especially need a warm, frost-free position.

• Climbing Tea roses: These are similar to the Noisettes, but with more of a Hybrid Tea appearance.

• Climbing Hybrid Tea: These have a Hybrid Tea nature and are usually sports (natural mutations) of Hybrid Teas.

• Climbing Bourbons: These are characterized by their Old rose type flowers. Like most other Climbers they have a repeat-flowering nature.

• Modern Climbers: This is a relatively new grouping. They have a repeat-flowering nature, with flowers resembling those of Hybrid Teas.

All of these can be pruned like those in Group Three.

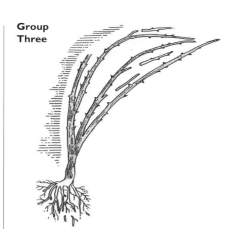

**Group Three**

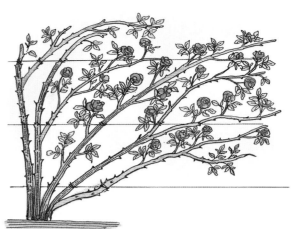

*1* During the dormant season, when a young Climber is received from a nursery, cut back coarse and uneven roots. Additionally, cut out weak shoots at their bases and lightly cut back the tips of unripe and damaged shoots. Then, plant it firmly and space out and loosely tie in the stems to create a permanent framework.

*2* During mid- and late summer of the following season, continue to tie in new shoots that develop from the existing framework, as well as those that grow from ground level. Also, train in strong shoots that develop from the main framework. The formation of this framework distinguishes Climbers from Ramblers, which each season replace stems that are cut out with fresh shoots from ground level. In the case of Climbers, a permanent framework is created. A few flowers will appear at the ends of new shoots. As soon as the flowers fade, cut them off. Do not be disappointed if only a few flowers appear; it is more important to build up the plant's framework.

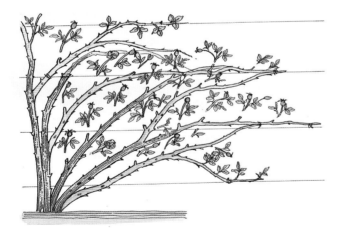

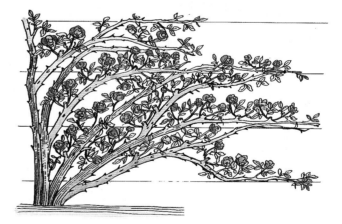

*3* From between mid-autumn of the same year and early spring of the following one, cut back all lateral shoots that have borne flowers to within three or four eyes of their points of origin. Additionally, cut out weak and diseased shoots and tie in leading shoots to the framework. Thin and weak shoots arising from the Climber's base should also be cut out. If pruning is left until early spring, also cut out frost-damaged shoots, especially from slightly tender varieties which have been given a too cold or wind-exposed position. Loose shoots that repeatedly flap against supports may also be damaged: check all loose shoots and cut them out as necessary.

*4* During the following mid- and late summer, flowers are borne on the tips of new growths as well as on lateral shoots. When the flowers fade, cut them off. Also tie in new shoots as they grow. Later in the same season, from mid-autumn to early spring, cut back all lateral shoots that have borne flowers to three or four eyes of their point of origin. At the same time, cut out weak and diseased shoots and tie in to a supporting framework of leading shoots.

The pruning and training activities detailed here should be repeated each year: completely cut out old and exhausted stems to within a few inches of the Climber's base to encourage fresh, strong growths to develop.

# PRUNING SPECIES AND SHRUB ROSES

Species and Shrub roses are increasingly capturing the attention of rose specialists as well as people new to gardening. These are roses with a more natural appearance than modern types, such as Hybrid Teas and Floribundas, and are ideal for planting in shrub or mixed borders where informality is desired. They include many that are native to various parts of the northern hemisphere – Europe, North America and Asia – as well as natural and cultivated crosses between two species.

Because many of these roses have been growing for thousands of years without interference from gardeners and horticulturalists, it is often suggested that they should be left alone to follow their own habits and to grow naturally. This may suit some of them, but certainly not all. By careful pruning, it is possible to prevent them becoming congested with unwanted growth and thereby to give them a longer and more floriferous lifespan.

**PRUNING GROUPS**

It may be thought that all Species and Shrub roses have the same nature and therefore need similar pruning techniques, but nothing could be further from the truth. For the convenience of gardeners, however, it is possible to simplify the pruning of these roses by categorizing them into three groups – although there are many types that do not fit into this classification.

**Group One** includes:
* Species roses (but not climbers) and their close hybrids.
* Japanese or Ramanas rose (*R. rugosa*) and hybrids.
* Burnet rose (*R. spinosissima*) and hybrids.
* The French rose (*R. gallica*).
* Hybrid Musks.

**INITIAL PRUNING**

When being planted, cut off coarse and weak roots. Also, shorten damaged and unripe shoots. During the first and second years, cut out a few old shoots in winter.

**Pruning Group One**

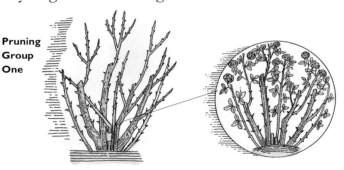

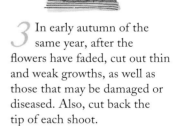

*1* During late winter or early spring of the second year, completely cut off shoots that have developed from the plant's base and are badly positioned. Also, cut back the tips of vigorous shoots.

*2* During the subsequent summer, the plant will produce flowers on shoots borne on old wood. At the same time, strong, new shoots will develop directly from the shrub's base.

*3* In early autumn of the same year, after the flowers have faded, cut out thin and weak growths, as well as those that may be damaged or diseased. Also, cut back the tip of each shoot.

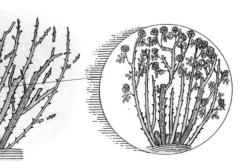

*4* During the third and subsequent years, regular pruning is essential. During late winter or early spring, cut back lateral shoots. Also, cut out at their bases one or two old shoots.

*5* In mid- and late summer of the same year the shrub will bear flowers on lateral shoots that have developed on the old shoots. During the same summer, fresh shoots will grow from the shrub's base.

*6* During early autumn, cut back the tips of shoots to encourage the development of laterals that will bear flowers during the following year. Cut out thin and weak shoots, and totally remove old ones.

**Group Two** includes: roses which flower chiefly on short lateral shoots as well as sub-laterals originating from two-year-old, or older, wood including:

- *R. × alba* types.
- Provence rose (*R. centifolia*) and its types.
- Moss roses.
- Most Damasks.
- Modern Shrub roses which have one main flush of bloom in mid-summer.

### INITIAL PRUNING
When being planted, cut off damaged and weak roots and lightly cut back the tips of diseased and thin shoots.

Rose 'Canary Bird' is a form of *Rosa xanthina* and creates an arching shrub which bears canary-yellow flowers during late spring and early summer.

**Pruning Group Two**

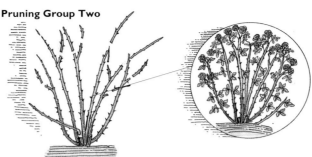

1 In late winter or early spring of the second year, cut back by about a third all those shoots that earlier developed from the shrub's base. Also, cut back to two or three eyes all laterals that developed on flowered shoots.

2 From mid-to late summer of the second year, flowers will be borne on lateral shoots that were cut back earlier. During this period, new shoots will be growing from the shrub's base. Cut off the flowers as they fade.

3 Slightly later, from early to late autumn of the second year, cut back shoots that are extra long. By doing this, the risk of the shrub being damaged or roots loosened by strong wind during late autumn and winter is reduced.

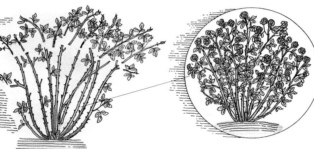

4 In late winter and early spring of the third and subsequent years, cut back by a third new shoots that developed from ground level. Also cut back laterals on flowered shoots to two or three eyes. Then cut out a few old shoots at the base.

5 From mid- to late summer of the same year, the bush will bear flowers on lateral shoots that were cut back earlier. The cycle of fresh shoots growing each year and later developing sideshoots which will bear flowers is repeated the following season.

6 Later in the season, from early to late autumn, cut off the ends of stems that are extra long. This reduces the area of stems and helps to prevent the shrub's roots being disturbed when shoots are blown by strong winds during late autumn and winter.

## GROUP THREE ROSES

Species and Shrub roses in this group include most China and Bourbon roses and many Modern Shrub types. Although they have a similar nature to those detailed in Group Two (ABOVE), they differ in that they flower recurrently throughout summer and into autumn both on the current season's shoots, and on laterals and sub-laterals that develop from both two-year and older shoots. Because many of the flowers are borne on laterals on old wood, these plants soon become congested if pruning is neglected. Therefore, regularly remove dead flowers and thin out twiggy clusters during summer. Also, encourage the development of fresh shoots from ground level by cutting out old ones during winter. At the same time, cut out all diseased shoots.

## GROUP ONE SPECIES AND SHRUB ROSES

Roses within this pruning group (*detailed on page 68*) include the Burnet rose, hybrid musks, Ramanas roses and the French rose. These roses have a dense, bushy nature, with flowers mainly on short lateral and sub-lateral shoots arising from two-year-old and older wood.

## THE BURNET ROSE

The Burnet rose is widely known as *Rosa Spinosissima*, but its botanically correct name is *R. pimpinellifolia*. It is also occasionally called the Scotch rose on account of hybrids and

ABOVE 'Buff Beauty', a Hybrid Musk, is well known for it sturdy growth, handsome foliage and large trusses of warm apricot-yellow flowers. It forms a shrub about 1.5m (5ft) high and wide.

varieties created and popularized by Scottish nurserymen as early as the beginning of the 1800s.

The Burnet rose is rarely more than 1.2m (4ft) high, with a suckering habit, and forms a thicket of erect, slender stems that bear small,

white, creamy-white or pale-pink flowers during late spring and early summer. Popular varieties include 'Grandiflora' (sometimes also known as 'Altaica' or *R. altaica*) with large, single, white flowers. 'Double White' has an exquisite charm, with lily-of-the-valley scented, double, globular, white heads. Known in Scotland as Prince Charlie's rose, 'Williams' Double Yellow' is slightly taller than

the species and often said to be related to the Austrian briar (*R. foetida*). It has double, heavily scented, deep-yellow blooms. In some earlier catalogues it was listed as 'Double Yellow'. 'William III' has a semi-double nature, with purplish-crimson flowers that fade to lilac-pink. 'Lutea Maxima' is a superb single yellow rose, with both the Austrian briar and the Burnet rose among its ancestors.

RIGHT 'Graham Thomas' is one of the English roses originated by David Austin Roses, and is named after the world-famous rosarian Graham Thomas. The pure yellow flowers have the fragrance of Tea roses. The plant grows about 1.2m (4ft) high and wide and creates an almost continuous display of flowers throughout the rose season.

'Roseraie de l'Hay' is a dense and vigorous shrub that grows to 1.8–2.1m (6–7ft).

'Double White' develops double, white flowers during early summer. It is scented like lily of the valley and grows to 60–90cm (2–3ft).

## HYBRID MUSKS

These have a graceful and refined nature with delicate colours and bear their flowers in large trusses. Varieties to consider include 'Ballerina' (hydrangea-like heads of single, blossom-pink flowers), 'Cornelia' (rosette-shaped blooms, coppery-apricot which fades to coppery-pink), 'Felicia' (strong-growing with silvery-pink flowers that deepen towards their centre) and 'Prosperity' (scented, large trusses of ivory-white, semi-double flowers).

LEFT 'Charles de Mills' is a strong-growing Gallica rose with large, rich crimson flowers that assume purple tints as they age. It forms a shrub about 1.5m (5ft) high and 1.2m (4ft) wide.

## RAMANAS ROSES

The Ramanas or Japanese rose (*R. rugosa*) has spawned many hardy, strong-growing and vibrantly-coloured varieties. They all are superb, but those of special merit include 'Agnes' (scented, rich yellow and amber flowers), 'Blanche Double de Coubert' (pure white and semi-double), 'Fru Dagmar Hastrup' (flesh-pink single flowers delicately veined

*Rosa gallica* 'Officinalis', widely known as the Apothecary's rose and red rose of Lancaster, develops large, semi-double, light-crimson flowers on shrubs about 1.2m (4ft) high and wide.

and with cream stamens), 'Lady Curzon' (rose-pink and single), 'Mrs Anthony Waterer' (richly fragrant and crimson), 'Roseraie de l'Hay' (strongly scented, with large, wine-purple buds that open to a glorious crimson-purple), 'Sarah Van Fleet' (slightly cupped, semi-double, mallow-pink flowers with cream stamens), 'Scabrosa' (large,

single, crimson flowers tinged with violet) and 'Snowdon' (a more recent introduction with fully double, rosette-like, pure white blooms).

Ramanas was said to be the Japanese name for this rose, but was mistaken for Hamanas, itself a corruption of *Hama-nashi*, 'Shore-pear'.

## THE FRENCH ROSE

Also known as the Provins and red rose, *R. gallica* is a suckering shrub with erect, bristly stems. It has many well-known forms including: 'Belle de Crécy' (rich cerise-pink flowers that slowly turn to soft parma-violet), 'Camaieux' (white, striped and splashed with crimson), 'Charles de Mills' (large, full-petalled, rich crimson flowers), 'Empress Joséphine' (large, clear-pink and veined in deep pink), 'Officinalis' (known as the Apothecary's rose and red rose of Lancaster, it has large, semi-double, light-crimson flowers), 'Tuscany' (dark maroon-crimson) and 'Tuscany Superb' (deep crimson, fading to light purple).

ABOVE *Rosa* 'Alba Maxima', an Alba rose, is also known as the Jacobite rose and develops masses of double, creamy-white flowers on shrubs about 1.8m (6ft) high and 1.5m (5ft) wide. The flowers often appear untidy.

### GROUP TWO SPECIES AND SHRUB ROSES

Roses in pruning Group Two (*detailed on page 69*) include several of the so-called Old roses, together with those Modern Shrub roses which have a main flush of flowers in mid-summer but are not repeat-flowering.

### OLD ROSES

These include the Albas and among these are 'Alba Maxima' (often known as the Jacobite rose, with double, creamy-white flowers that are first blush-pink), 'Celestial' (semi-double, sweetly scented and shell-pink), 'Félicité Parmentier' (slightly ball-shape, fresh pink and creamy at the edges), and 'Queen of Denmark' (strongly scented, large, quartered blooms of soft, glowing pink, with attractive, grey-green leaves).

### CENTIFOLIAS

Also known as Provence or cabbage roses, because they usually have large and globular, scented blooms. These include 'Chapeau de Napoléon' (often known as Crested Moss, with richly fragrant, pure pink flowers), 'Fantin-Latour' (cupped, later opening and curling backwards, blush-pink flowers that deepen to shell-pink at their centres), 'Robert le Diable' (purple-shaded with slate-grey, splashed with scarlet and cerise) and 'Tour de Malakoff' (large, open blooms, first magenta-purple, later parma-violet and then turning lavender and grey).

### DAMASKS

This group is said to have been brought from the Middle East by Crusaders. Most of them are fragrant and varieties to consider include 'Celsiana' (semi-double, soft-pink blooms with golden stamens), 'La Ville de Bruxelles' (fully double, rich pink, very fragrant flowers), 'Mme Hardy' (a superb rose, initially cupped and with white petals), 'Marie Louise' (very large and intense pink).

### MODERN SHRUB ROSES

Modern Shrub roses that have a main display in mid-summer, without the benefit of repeat flowering, include 'Cerise Bouquet' (semi-double, cerise-pink), 'Frühlingsgold' (pale yellow), 'Frühlings-morgen' (rose-pink) and 'Scarlet Fire' (scarlet).

### MOSS ROSES

These are closely related to the Provence or cabbage roses, more properly known as Centifolias, but have developed green moss-like growths on their sepals, the outer part of the flower. Popular in Victorian times, they are now represented by varieties such as 'Comtesse du Murinais' (full-petalled and blush-pink, deepening to salmon-pink), 'General Kleber' (large, flat and quartered, soft mauve-pink flowers), 'Gloire des Mousseux' (fragrant, clear pink blooms), 'Louis Gimard' (large, globular and cupped, light-crimson blooms with lilac tones), 'Réné d'Anjou' (fragrant and soft pink) and 'William Lobb' (known as the old velvet rose, with dark-crimson flowers that fade to violet-grey. The flowers are richly scented and it is ideal for planting in shrub borders).

*Rosa* 'Comtesse du Murinais', a Moss rose, forms a strong shrub about 1.8m (6ft) high and 1.2m (4ft) wide, with blush-pink flowers that become white when fully open.

ABOVE 'Cerise Bouquet', a Modern Shrub rose, is robust and arching, with cerise-pink flowers borne in large, open sprays. The flowers have the bouquet of raspberries. This is a robust shrub which grows about 2.4m (8ft) high and wide.

## GROUP THREE SPECIES AND SHRUB ROSES

Roses within this pruning group (detailed on page 69) include most of the China types, some Modern Shrub roses, many Bourbons and most Hybrid Perpetuals. They develop flowers on lateral and sub-lateral shoots.

## CHINA ROSES

These include 'Hermosa' (fragrant, globular, little pink flowers), 'Mutabilis' (pointed, flame-coloured buds that open to reveal coppery-yellow, single flowers changing to pink and, finally, coppery-crimson), 'Old Blush China' (also known as the monthly rose, it develops graceful clusters of pale-pink flowers through most of summer and well into autumn) and 'Sophie's Perpetual' (sprays of small, deep-pink flowers). China roses are usually slightly tender and best planted in frost-free positions.

## BOURBON TYPES

The result of crossing China roses with Portland types. They usually have a rich fragrance, and varieties in this group include 'Mme Isaac Pereire' (vigorous, with large madder-crimson flowers and a rich fragrance) and 'Zéphirine Drouhin' (a Bourbon climber with a glorious fragrance, thornless stems and bright, carmine-pink, semi-double flowers).

## HYBRID PERPETUALS

Very popular in Victorian and Edwardian times and robust forms of these roses can be put into pruning Group Three. Examples include 'Baron Girod de l'Ain' (dark-crimson flowers, cup-shaped at first but later opening wide), 'Baronne Prévost' (rose-pink), 'Gloire de Ducher' (large, deep-crimson, fragrant flowers that slowly become purple) and 'Reine des Violettes' (shades of lilac and purple, with greyish foliage).

'Fantin-Latour' forms a shrub about 1.8m (6ft) high and 1.5m (5ft) wide. During mid-summer it produces fragrant, blush-coloured flowers.

ABOVE *Rosa* 'Captain Hayward', a Hybrid Perpetual, has extremely deep-pink flowers borne amid green leaves.

ABOVE *Rosa* 'Ferdinand Pichard', a Hybrid Perpetual, has globular, pink flowers striped with purple and crimson. They are fragrant and borne on shrubs about 1.2m (4ft) high and 90cm (3ft) wide.

*Rosa* 'Robert de Diable' (left) has purple-shaded flowers splashed with scarlet and cerise, while 'Tour de Malakoff' (right) reveals flowers first magenta-purple, then turning through parma-violet to lavender and grey. Both these roses are Centifolia types.

# FRUIT TREES, BUSHES AND CANES

Fruit gardens in temperate countries yield as many succulent fruits as those in tropical regions, with the benefit of many of them having a longer storage life. This is especially true of apples, some varieties of which, although picked in late summer and autumn of one year, can be stored for eating well into the following year. To encourage the annual production of fruit on trees, bushes and canes, yearly pruning is essential and is especially needed where fruit trees are trained to grow against walls or alongside frameworks of supporting wires. Growing tree fruits at 45-degree angles or on horizontal branches encourages earlier fruiting than growing them in a bush shape, but special pruning is needed .

Bush fruits such as gooseberries, blackcurrants, red and white currants, need yearly attention: some of these bear fruits mainly on shoots produced from the plant's base during the previous year; others have a more permanent framework.

### IS PRUNING NECESSARY?

Experiments with apple trees indicate that an unpruned tree will bear fruits long before one that is pruned and trained to form a framework of branches. But if trees are neglected and left unpruned for long, the quality, quantity and size of the fruits declines rapidly. The bush or tree becomes cluttered with branches and shoots, each intruding upon its neighbour's space and preventing the entry of light and air. Pests and diseases are also encouraged by a conglomeration of shoots. Pruning during the plant's early years is designed to create a framework of well-spaced, stout branches. Once this has been achieved, the emphasis changes to the regular production of fruit.

Other reasons for pruning apple and pear trees is to control a tree's vigour, to remove pest- and disease-damaged shoots, thin out clusters of fruit spurs, and to

ABOVE and OPPOSITE Pear and apple blossom. Nature naturally regulates the number of fruits that apple trees bear. During early summer, there is usually a shedding of fruitlets. With some varieties, the fruitlets are thinned by the grower who removes those that are misshapen or have been attacked by pests or diseases. This task is left until after the so-called mid-summer 'drop', which naturally discards fruitlets. Some varieties also shed fruits just prior to picking time; this is known as 'Pre-harvest drop'. Fruit trees, when in flower, are very attractive.

counteract the tendency of some trees to bear more fruits one year than in the following one; this is widely known as biennial bearing.

If cordon, espalier and fan-trained trees are neglected for a few years, it may be impossible to return them to their earlier and more tidy shape.

### BUSHES AND CANES

These, too, need regular pruning. If neglected they soon become a jungle of shoots, accompanied by a rapid decrease in the quality and amount of the fruits. Cane fruits such as raspberries, and especially the more vigorous hybrid berries, become a mixture of old and fruited shoots and weak, spindly new ones. The yearly removal of old canes encourages the development of young, healthy ones. Blackcurrant bushes also become congested when neglected, producing a mass of old, unfruitful stems.

# PRUNING FRUIT TREES AND BUSHES

Pruning established fruit trees mainly involves the use of secateurs, but if the tree is excessively large and unfruitful other techniques have to be employed. These include bark-ringing and root-pruning, which are both old methods but still usable for tackling a large, unproductive tree. Nicking and notching is another unusual practice but ideal for use on cordon and espalier apple trees trained against a wall. It is used to encourage or deter the development of shoots and to ensure they grow in the right direction.

With all fruit trees, soft-fruit bushes and cane fruits, it is essential to begin to prune them soon after they are planted. Some, such as blackcurrant bushes, are pruned immediately they are planted, whereas others should be pruned within the same dormant season. There is no substitute for careful pruning during a plant's formative period. For this reason, the sequence of pruning, throughout this fruit-growing chapter, begins with a young, newly planted tree, bush or cane.

### APPLES AND PEARS

In large-scale orchards, where these fruits are grown as bushes, half-standards and standards, they are invariably pruned only in winter. In gardens, however, and especially where they are grown as espaliers and cordons, they are pruned in both winter and summer. Occasionally, trees that are heavily pruned in summer become infested with woolly aphids (sometimes known as American blight). Winter-pruning is normally carried out during a tree's dormant period, but it can be delayed and performed after buds begin to swell. However, late pruning often checks subsequent growth – although this reaction can sometimes be used to advantage when pruning excessively vigorous trees.

**Summer pruning**
Once a tree's framework and shape are established, specially trained trees, such as cordons and espaliers, can be summer-pruned. The removal of shoots and leaves during summer checks the growth of roots and reduces the development of shoots. It also leads to the formation of fruit buds at the base of the shoot that has been pruned. Use sharp secateurs when summer-pruning.

**Winter pruning**
This is performed during a tree's dormant period and has several purposes: to direct the growth of a tree into branch and shoot development; prevent the overcrowding of branches and lateral shoots; and to regulate the number and position of fruit buds that subsequently develop and produce flowers and fruit. Leading shoots can also be ensured.

## NICKING AND NOTCHING

This is a technique sometimes performed on apple and pear trees. Nicking is the removal of a piece of horseshoe-shaped bark immediately below a bud. This reduces the flow of sap to it and prevents the bud's development. Notching is where a piece of bark directly above a bud is removed, thereby encouraging the bud to develop. Both nicking and notching are performed in late spring, when the sap is starting to flow.

**Notching**
Use a sharp knife to make a horizontal cut, about 3mm (⅛ in) deep and 6mm (¼ in) above the bud. Then cut out a wedge shape by slicing towards it at a 45-degree angle. Carefully remove the small wedge of wood.

**Nicking**
Use a sharp knife and make a 3mm (⅛ in) deep cut 6mm (¼ in) below the bud. Make a further cut, at a 45-degree angle, so that a wedge of wood can be removed. With both notching and nicking, do not damage the bud.

## BARK-RINGING

A technique used to encourage an excessively vigorous tree to produce fruit, rather than shoots. It is only suitable for use on apple trees and is regarded as a last resort to induce fruiting. Modern dwarf rootstocks have reduced the need for this technique, but it encourages more blossom to set and improves the quality of dessert varieties. Bark-ring trees at blossom time.

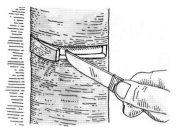

*1* Use a sharp knife to cut just under the bark. Make two cuts, 6–12mm (¹/₄–¹/₂in) apart. Ensure that they are parallel with each other and about 15cm (6in) below the lowest branch.

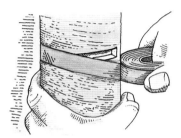

*2* Remove the bark between the two cuts, ensuring that the cut area is not widened. If it is too wide, there is a chance that the tree will be killed; if too narrow, it is ineffective.

*3* Do not paint the wound. Instead, wind several layers of adhesive tape over the cut area. Once a callus has formed over the cut, the tape can be removed, usually by the latter part of mid-summer.

## ROOT-PRUNING

This is a way to encourage apple trees that are growing too strongly and producing masses of shoots and no fruit buds to start bearing fruits. It should be tried only after other methods have failed, such as pruning the tree lightly and creating a grassy sward all around the tree's base.

During late autumn and early winter, dig a trench 30–38cm (12–15in) deep in a complete circle 90cm–1.2m (3–4ft) from the trunk. Use a saw or secateurs to sever all exposed roots, then refill and firm soil in the trench. For large trees, tackle this task over two winters, half one year and half the following season.

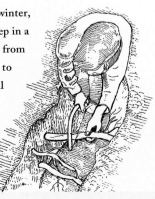

## SHAPES AND SIZES

Fruit gardens are a medley of trees, bushes and canes, some with a permanent framework, others with a woody structure that is replaced each year. Most of these plants are free-standing, creating bushes or trees with only a single stake to support them. Others, such as cordons, espaliers and fans, need tiered wires strained between posts or secured to a wall. Because space in most gardens is limited, few standard and half-standard apple and pear trees are now planted; instead, bushes or forms trained against walls are more popular.

Blackcurrants develop fresh stems from their bases to replace those that produced fruits. Old stems are removed in autumn.

Gooseberries, red and white currants form a framework of shoots from a permanent 'leg' connecting the roots with the branches.

Raspberries, blackberries and hybrid berries produce fruits on canes which are trained on supports of tiered wires.

Apples and pears can be grown as bushes which have a short trunk, 60–90cm (2–3ft) long.

Apples and pears, as well as cherries and plums, can be grown as standards and half-standards.

Many fruits are suitable for growing as espaliers, when they can be grown against walls.

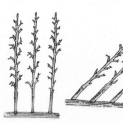

Apples and pears can be grown as vertical cordons. These do not bear fruit as quickly as those grown at an angle.

Apples and pears are widely grown as cordons, where the stems are trained at an angle. Double cordons are popular.

Cherries, peaches and nectarines are often grown as fans, with radiating stems. Careful pruning is essential.

# PRUNING APPLES AND PEARS

Pruning apples and pears is an important operation and if wrongly performed may spoil the tree's shape and seriously delay the time when it begins to bear fruit. The initial purpose of pruning is to build up the shape or form of the tree, whether it is a bush, pyramid, cordon or espalier. Unless there is a strong, permanent framework of well-spaced branches, large crops of high-quality fruits cannot be produced. Creating a permanent framework may take four or five years if a maiden plant (one-year-old and with a single stem) is planted – but it is a task that cannot be rushed. The second purpose of pruning is to encourage the development of fruit buds and to regulate their number and positions.

ABOVE Apples and pears can be grown on bushes and trees of varying size and shape. Here, the dessert apple variety 'Wagener' is grown as a dwarf pyramid.

**SPUR- OR TIP-BEARING?**
Apple varieties can be classified into two main types: spur-bearing types that bear fruits mainly on fruit buds on short spurs close to the branch, and those known as tip-bearing types that produce fruits on fruit buds on or near the tips of shoots. There are some varieties that bear fruit in both of these styles. The technique for pruning apple and pear varieties with these characteristics is detailed on pages 82 and 83.
✳ Spur-fruiting varieties include: 'American Mother'

'Conference'
(dessert variety)

'Beth' (dessert variety)

'Egremont Russet'
(dessert variety)

'Cox's Orange Pippin'
(dessert variety)

(D), 'Ashmead Kernel' (D), 'Crispin' (D), 'Cox's Orange Pippin' (D), 'Discovery' (D), 'Egremont Russet' (D), 'Ellison's Orange' (D), 'Epicure' (D), 'George Neal' (C), 'Golden Delicious' (D), 'Grenadier' (C), 'Howgate Wonder' (C), 'Idared' (D), 'James Grieve' (D), 'Kidd's Orange Red' (D), 'Lane's Prince Albert' (C), 'Laxton's Fortune' (D), 'Merton Knave' (D), 'Orleans Reinette' (D), 'Ribston Pippin' (D), 'Sunset' (D) and 'Tydeman's Late Orange' (D)
✳ Tip-bearing varieties include: 'Beauty of Bath' (D), 'Irish Peach' (D) and 'Worcester Pearmain' (D)
✳ Tip/spur-bearing varieties include: 'Bramley Seedling' (C), 'George Cave' (D), 'Golden Noble' (C), 'Lord Lambourne' (D) and 'St Edmund's Russet' (D)
[C = *Culinary*
D = *Dessert*]

Pear varieties can also be grouped according to where they bear their fruits, although most of the dessert types tend to develop them on spurs. The exceptions are 'Jargonelle' and 'Joséphine de Malines', which are tip-bearing.

ABOVE Espalier fruit trees need support from galvanized wires strained between strong posts. This is an ideal way to grow apples and pears in a small garden.

LEFT Cordon-trained trees are usually formed of a single stem grown at an angle. This encourages the early development of fruits and is another excellent way to train apple and pear trees in a small area.

Pear 'Beurre Bedford' is a succulent dessert variety.

Apple 'Laxton Fortune', a dessert variety, bears red-striped yellow fruits with very sweet flesh.

Pear 'Doyenne du Comice' is ideal for storing for winter eating. The fruits are small and tender, with juicy flesh.

Apple 'Brownlees Russet' is a superbly-flavoured dessert variety.

Apple 'Bramley's Seedling' is one of the best-known cooking varieties. The fruits are large and green-yellow.

'Lane's Prince Albert' is a culinary variety, yellow-green with red streaks, and soft flesh.

# APPLES AND PEARS
## *Formative Pruning*

Apples and pears are the most popular tree fruits in temperate regions, each year reliably producing large crops. The range of varieties is wide; there are estimated to be more than six thousand apples varieties. Several generations ago most apples and pears were grown on trees 3.6m (12ft) or more high. They were difficult to prune and perilous when the fruits were picked – three-legged fruit ladders were used and when the pickers reached the top, they needed supreme gymnastic abilities to stay aloft safely! Today, there are smaller forms and the most popular ones for ordinary gardens are bushes, cordons and espaliers.

Although it is possible to buy bush-trained trees that are two or even three years old, one-year-old plants, known as maidens, can be bought and trained. For this reason, formative training begins during the first winter and with a maiden tree. Another term for them is 'whips', as they are formed of a single stem. In addition to buying and planting bare-rooted trees from late autumn to late winter, both one- and two-year-old trees can be bought growing in containers. In this form they can be planted at any time during the year, whenever the soil is not frozen or waterlogged.

**TRAINING BUSHES**

Bush-shaped trees are popular ways to grow apples and pears, enabling easy pruning and the fruits to be picked without having to resort to ladders. Bushes have stems 60–90cm (2–3ft) long, with branches arising fairly closely together. There are both dwarf bush forms and normal bushes: always select the type that suits the size of your garden.

- Dwarf bushes are planted 2.4–4.5m (8–15ft) apart in rows similarly spaced; apple varieties yield 13.5–22.5kg (30–50lb) and pears 9–13.5kg (20–30lb).
- Ordinary bushes are planted 3.6–4.5m (12–15ft) apart in rows similarly spaced; apple varieties yield 27–54kg (60–120lb) and pears 18–43kg (40–100lb).

before

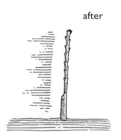

after

---

### OTHER TREE FORMS

In addition to bush, cordon and espalier-trained trees, there are several others: half-standard 1.2–1.3m (4–4½ ft) trunk, and standard 1.8–2.1m (6–7ft) trunk. These are initially slow to bear fruits, but eventually the yield is heavy. Dwarf pyramids are popular and as they grow only 2.1m (7ft) high and with a 1.2m (4ft) spread are ideal for small gardens. Fan-trained trees are also popular; train against a high wall.

*1* From late autumn to late winter, plant bare-rooted one-year-old trees (maidens). These will have a single stem without any sideshoots. When two-year-old trees (sometimes known as feathered maidens) are planted, pruning then begins as detailed in the first two drawings on the opposite page. Take care not to knock or excessively stain the graft or the area around it.

*2* Prune the one-year-old tree in winter when it is dormant and whenever the air temperature is above freezing. When creating a dwarf bush shape, cut the stem back to 60cm (2ft) above the soil, severing just above a healthy bud. When an ordinary bush is being created, cut 75cm (2½ ft) above soil level. Cutting the stem in this way stimulates growth.

before

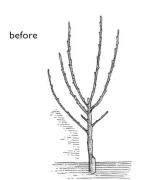

after

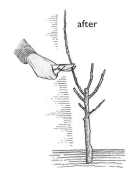

*3* By the following winter, the two-year-old plant will have developed several strong stems that grow upwards. Preferably, the bush should have shoots that form wide angles with the main stem, as these ensure a stronger joint than ones that form narrow angles and are close to the stem. Additionally, some shoots will be growing from lower down on the stem.

*4* Select four of the strongest, healthiest shoots to form the main framework and cut them back by two-thirds. Ensure they are well spaced out. Prune each of them to just above a healthy, outward-facing bud. Also cut out all unwanted shoots flush with the main stem. The prunings cannot be composted, so collect and burn them as soon as possible.

### DIFFERENCES BETWEEN APPLES AND PEARS

Pears develop their blossom slightly earlier in a season than apples and therefore are more likely to be damaged by late spring frosts. Consequently they benefit from a warm, sheltered position. Because they flower before apples, the summer pruning of pears takes place about a week earlier than it does for apples. The pruning of pears is much the same as for apples, although during a tree's formative period pears are best pruned less vigorously. Once they start to bear fruits, pear trees can be pruned more severely than apples, both when cutting back the tips of leading shoots and when shortening lateral ones. Indeed, pears develop fruit spurs more readily than apples, with the result that more attention is needed during subsequent years to thinning them out. If thinning is neglected, the fruits will eventually be small and of poor quality.

before

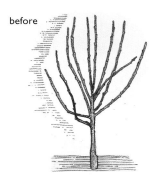

after

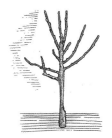

before

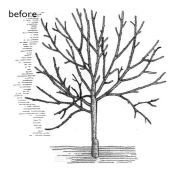

after

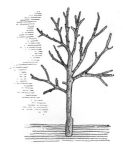

*5* By the following winter, the three-year-old bush will have developed many shoots. Some of these will be extensions of the shoots pruned back by two-thirds during the previous winter, while others will arise from the trunk. The thickness and vigour of these stems depends on the previous season's pruning; if shoots were only lightly tipped, subsequent extensions of them will be thin and pliable and unable to support heavy crops of fruits later on during later years.

*6* During winter, again cut back all leading shoots by about two-thirds of their length. Always cut them to just above an outward-pointing bud. Completely cut out damaged shoots, as well as those that cross the top of the bush. Small lateral shoots should be cut back to three buds long to encourage the formation of fruiting spurs. By this time, the bush's head will be starting to form and the main framework can be seen. Correct pruning at this stage ensures a strong framework.

*7* By the following winter, the four-year-old bush will have grown dramatically during the previous summer and will now have several leading shoots as well as younger, slender sideshoots. The severity of winter-pruning influences subsequent growth and development of fruit: the greater the proportion of wood removed during pruning, the more vigorous will be the following year's growth and the smaller will be the crop of fruit it produces. Nevertheless, strong branches are essential.

*8* In winter, shorten the leading shoots by a third to a half, depending on the bush's vigour. Cut back lateral shoots that are growing on the insides of the branches and towards the bush's centre to about 10cm (4in) long. Prune out dead and crossing shoots. The early development of fruits can be encouraged by leaving some of the long, lower shoots unpruned, but the development of a strong framework is imperative. Pick up and burn all shoots in case they are diseased.

# APPLES AND PEARS
## *Established Trees*

Once an apple or pear tree is beyond its formative years (see pages 80 and 81 for initial pruning, when the purpose of pruning is to form a framework of evenly spaced, strong branches), pruning assumes a different role. Its purpose is then to encourage the formation of fruit buds and to ensure they are evenly positioned throughout the tree. There is also often a need to regulate a tree's vigour, although primarily it is the choice of the rootstock that controls this. On very fertile soils, trees can develop excessively vigorous growth. The first step to control this is to grass below the tree, depriving it of much of the nitrogen it was receiving and thereby reducing vegetative growth. Vigorous winter-pruning encourages growth and in such a case summer-pruning is useful (*see opposite page*).

Before winter-pruning, establish if the tree bears its fruit mainly on spurs or along the tip of shoots. The fruiting nature of many popular varieties is detailed on pages 78 and 79.

### BIENNIAL BEARING

Some apple varieties, such as 'Blenheim Orange', 'Bramley's Seedling' and 'Laxton's Superb', bear a heavier crop one year than another. One way to even out this problem is to take action in the spring, before a heavy crop is expected. Rub half to three-quarters of the fruit buds from each spur, leaving only one or two fruiting buds on each. Biennial bearing is less of a problem with pears.

**Spur-bearing apple tree**

*1* Once an apple tree is established, the objective when pruning spur-bearing varieties must be to encourage the regular development of spurs along each branch.

before

*2* During winter, when the tree is dormant, shorten lateral shoots to just above three or four buds from their bases. Also, shorten to one bud long laterals that were pruned the previous year. Prune back the leader shoot to half of the growth produced during the previous year. Cut to an upward-pointing bud.

after

**Tip-bearing apple tree**

before

after

*1* Tip-bearing apple varieties bear most of their fruits towards the ends of shoots. Therefore, the purpose of pruning is to encourage the development of young shoots. For this reason, leave short lateral shoots unpruned, so that they develop fruit buds at their tips; they can be pruned back in later years. Some apple varieties bear fruits both on spurs and towards the tips of shoots; these are best treated as spur-bearing types.

*2* Cut back leading shoots by about a third, severing them just above a healthy, upward-pointing bud. Leave all but the most vigorous lateral shoots unpruned, but cut back by half any that are more than 23cm (9in) long. Cut them to leave a bud pointing in the desired direction. The short laterals that are unpruned will develop fruit spurs. Also, cut back to one bud those shoots which are growing from laterals.

## CONTROLLING EXCESSIVE VIGOUR

There are four main ways to control excessive vigour – apart from the selection of a dwarfing rootstock. One is to rake the soil level around the tree in spring and then to dust the surface with grass seed and to lightly rake it in. Use fine grasses, as coarse ones tend to restrict growth too much. Summer-pruning trees (*below, right*) is another method. Root-pruning and bark-ringing are further methods, and these are described and illustrated on page 77.

**Thinning out spurs**

before

after

*1* After several years, branches of varieties that bear their fruits on spurs often become too numerous, forming complicated patterns. Because of the congestion, the quality and size of their fruits diminishes. The branch shown above needs thinning.

*2* During winter, use sharp secateurs to thin out a few spurs and to remove others completely. Ensure that the remaining spurs are equally spaced. As well as concentrating the tree's energies into fewer spurs, more light and air can enter the tree.

**Replacement shoots**

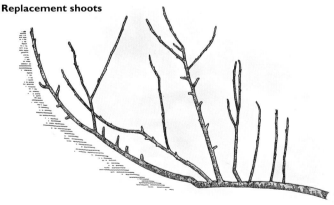

*1* During a tree's life, branches are continually being bent downwards by the weight of fruit. It is therefore essential to ensure that each branch has at least one shoot further back from the tip that can replace the end which is bent down, to prevent branches trailing on the ground.

*2* During winter pruning, ensure a suitable replacement shoot, growing upwards and on the upperside of a branch, is not removed. If the branch's tip is weighed down, cut it back to this replacement shoot. In its turn, this shoot will also need replacement.

### THINNING APPLES AND PEARS

**The purpose in thinning fruits is to produce better quality fruits. During early summer, bend over and snap off badly formed fruits, but leave the stalks behind. Later, during mid-summer, use sharp scissors or pointed secateurs to thin dessert apples, leaving one or two in each cluster spaced 10–15cm (4–6in) apart; for culinary apples, space them 15–20cm (6–8in) apart. Pears need less thinning, so leave two fruits on each cluster.**

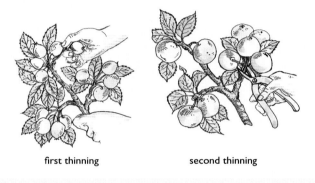

first thinning

second thinning

**Summer-pruning**

*1* Summer-pruning of apple and pear trees grown as bushes is not essential (as opposed to trained forms such as cordons, espaliers and fans, where pruning in summer is a vital part of their training). However, it encourages the development of high-quality fruits and checks excessive growth. Cut back lateral shoots when their bases become woody, some time in late summer, to about 13cm (5in) from their bases.

*2* If shoots are growing from these sideshoots, trim them to just above one leaf from their bases. Do not prune the leading shoot on each branch; it will be pruned later in winter. As well as improving the quality of the fruits, removing all this growth enables light and air to enter the tree to ripen the shoots and buds. It also improves the colour of the fruits. While doing this job, inspect the leaves and stems for diseases.

# APPLES AND PEARS
## *Cordons and Espaliers*

Both apples and pears, when grown as cordons and espaliers, are ideal in small gardens. They can be planted in the open garden or against a wall. Both of these 'trained' forms need support from tiers of galvanized wires. The training and pruning information for these fruits that follows is for starting with a one-year-old tree. This would have been grafted during the previous year. It is also possible to buy two- or three-year-old trees, but ensure they are properly shaped and have plenty of fruiting spurs. However, it is more difficult to match a partly-trained tree to an existing framework of supporting wires than to start with a young plant. A young plant also has the advantage of being transplanted more easily than one a few years older, and becomes established far more quickly.

There are several apple rootstocks used for both cordons and espaliers, but in a small garden M9 is best. For pears, Quince A or C rootstocks are suitable.

### CORDONS

These are formed of a single, straight stem, grown at an angle of 45 degrees and covered with spurs that bear fruits. Some cordons are grown vertically, but this is unusual as they grow higher and do not develop fruits as early as those planted obliquely. Some are grown as a single stem, others with two and, occasionally, three vertical branches.

Cordons are mostly pruned during summer, except in areas of high rainfall where masses of secondary shoots develop after summer-pruning. It is best to winter-prune neglected cordons initially, with a return to summer-pruning later. As well as cutting back sideshoots to about 2.5cm (1in) of the main stem, thin out excessively long and tightly-clustered spurs (*see page 85*).

Pruning in winter is also a good way to stimulate a cordon's growth when it is failing to grow strongly enough.

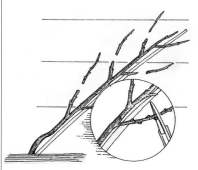

1 During the dormant season, from late autumn to late winter, plant maiden trees, 75cm (2½ ft) apart and at 45-degree angles by the side of tiers of supporting wires, 60cm (2ft), 1.2m (4ft) and 1.8m (6ft) above the ground. Additionally, insert a 2.4m (8ft) long, strong bamboo cane slightly under the 45-degree stem: tie the bamboo cane to the supporting wires, then the stem to the cane.

Do not prune the leading shoot, but cut back lateral shoots to within three or four buds of their base. Do not prune laterals that are shorter than this. Cut above a bud.

2 In the spring of the following year, leaves and blossom will begin to develop from the cut-back lateral shoots. Do not let cordons bear fruits during their first growing season: remove the blossom, but take care not to damage the growth bud just behind it. By mid-summer of the same year, young shoots will have developed from the cut-back laterals: they must be cut back to one leaf beyond the base cluster. Cut back to three leaves from their base all shoots growing directly from the main stem (*above*). Check that the stem is secure, but not constricted.

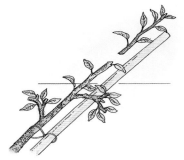

3 In late summer of the same year, just before the leaves fall off the plant, cut back further growth that has grown from shoots pruned back earlier. Prune it back to mature wood. Areas of high rainfall often encourage the development of masses of secondary growth late in summer. If this repeatedly happens, resort to winter-pruning. At this stage, do not cut back the leading shoot. In late spring of the following year, cut back the leading shoot when it has passed the top wire (*above*). At this stage, the cordon's top will be about 2.1m (7ft) high.

## THINNING SPURS

The clusters of spurs on cordons eventually become congested and produce only small fruits. At any time from late autumn to late winter they can be thinned out. Use sharp secateurs to cut out buds that are weak and on the underside, or markedly shaded by the branch. Thin out long, overlapping spurs to two or three fruit buds.

before          after

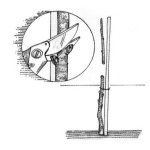

*1* To create an espalier, plant a maiden apple or pear tree during winter. Then, cut back the stem to a healthy bud just above the bottom wire. There should also be two other healthy buds positioned immediately below it.

*2* From early to late summer, the top three buds will grow. Loosely but firmly, tie the leading shoots to a vertical cane, and the two sideshoots to two others at angles of 45 degrees. The canes are tied to the wires.

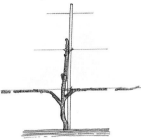

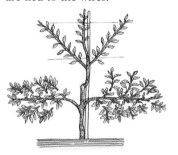

*3* During the following winter, cut off the leading shoot just above the next wire. Shoots will develop to form the next tier. Lower the two side branches and shorten them by a third to a healthy, strong, downward-pointing bud.

*4* During summer, secure the leading and two top sideshoots to canes. Cut off shoots growing between the first and second tier to three leaves long. Prune sideshoots on the bottom tier to three or four leaves long.

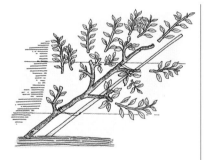

*4* When the cordon is established, during mid-summer of each year cut back the leading shoot to leave about 2.5cm (1in) of new growth. Also, prune back all mature lateral shoots that are growing from the main stem and are longer than 23cm (9in) to three leaves from their points of origin. Cut back shoots that are growing from existing spurs and sideshoots to one leaf beyond the rosette of leaves at their base. Do not include leaves that form a basal cluster in this number. Check that the main stem is firmly, but not too tightly, secured.

### ESPALIERS

This type of tree takes longer to create than cordons. It is formed of a central stem, from which rise tiers of horizontal stems 38–45cm (15–18in) apart. Support them on galvanized wires strained between strong posts.

Build up the tiers in a systematic manner, as illustrated and described. As well as ensuring each tier is formed, build up fruiting spurs on the lower ones by cutting back laterals to three leaves above the base cluster. On the tier below that, cut back sub-laterals to one leaf.

If, during summer, one side of a tier is growing faster than the other one, lower it slightly. Conversely, if it is much smaller than its twin, raise it.

Once the tiers are formed and their ends have been cut back to fit the allotted space, prune them in the same way as for cordons (*see left*).

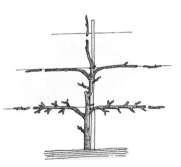

*5* During subsequent winters, form further tiers in the same way as detailed earlier. Lower the tier created in summer and cut it back by a third. Also, tip back the shoots on the lower tier.

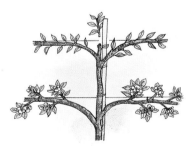

*6* During early summer, when the top wire is reached, cut off the leading shoot. When the arms fill the wires, cut off their ends. Cut back sideshoots to three leaves; sub-laterals to one leaf.

# PLUMS AND GAGES
## Bushes, Pyramids and Standards

Once established, plums and gages grown as bushes, pyramids and half-standards require little pruning, although attention is always needed in spring to remove dead, crossing and rubbing branches. Plums and gages are not suitable for growing as espaliers and cordons, although they are often cultivated as fan-trained trees against a warm wall. When grown as fans, their training and pruning for the first few years is the same as for fan-trained peaches (*see pages 90 and 91*). Thereafter, in spring rub out shoots growing towards the wall and in mid-summer pinch out the tips of young shoots not required for the framework; they later become fruiting spurs. After cropping, cut back these pinched-back shoots to three leaves.

Many plum and gage trees are planted as 'bare-rooted' plants and are best put into the ground during late autumn or early winter. They are also sold as 'container-grown' plants and can be planted at any time of the year when the soil is not frozen or waterlogged.

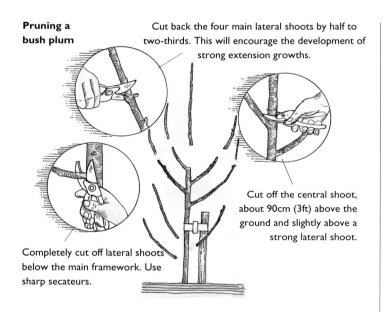

**Pruning a bush plum**

Cut back the four main lateral shoots by half to two-thirds. This will encourage the development of strong extension growths.

Cut off the central shoot, about 90cm (3ft) above the ground and slightly above a strong lateral shoot.

Completely cut off lateral shoots below the main framework. Use sharp secateurs.

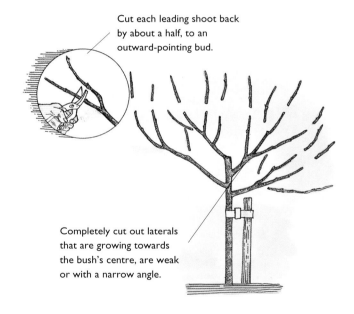

Cut each leading shoot back by about a half, to an outward-pointing bud.

Completely cut out laterals that are growing towards the bush's centre, are weak or with a narrow angle.

1 Plant a two-year-old (feathered maiden) tree in late autumn or early winter. Do not plant it in late winter as growth often begins in early spring. Securely stake the tree to prevent the roots being rocked in the soil. Start pruning a bush plum in late winter or early spring when growth begins and the buds start to break. Cut the central stem about 90cm (3ft) above the ground and slightly above a sideshoot. There should be three strong shoots below it. With each of these main shoots, prune them back by half to two-thirds, severing them just above an outward-facing bud. Then cut off, flush with the main stem, all sideshoots below the top four shoots.

2 In early spring of the following year, again prune the bush. At this stage it will be three years old. The lateral shoots that were pruned back during the previous year will have produced extension growths. Prune these back by about half. At the same time, cut out at their bases all other shoots growing from the main shoots. At this stage, the bush will have about eight, well-spaced and strong stems. During the following years, little pruning is needed, other than cutting out dead or crossing branches in summer. Remove suckers from the ground and cut off shoots that are growing from the trunk and below the lowest main branch. Regularly check that the bush is securely staked.

**SILVER LEAF DISEASE**

This is a notorious disease of members of the Rosaceae family and mainly attacks plums, gages, damsons and cherries. Apples and pears can also be affected, but not so often. Disease spores enter wounds, causing silver discoloration of the leaves and, eventually, the branches to die back. Entry of the spores into plums and other 'stone' fruits can be prevented by pruning them only when the sap is rising. Coat any large cuts with a fungicidal wound-sealing paint.

**Pruning a pyramid tree**

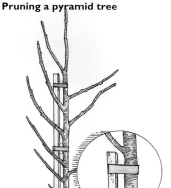

*1* Pyramid trees differ from bush shapes in producing sideshoots (laterals) over a much longer part of the trunk. Plant a dormant, two-year-old tree (feathered maiden) in late autumn or early winter. Use tree-ties to secure the stem.

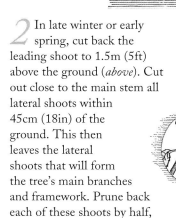

*2* In late winter or early spring, cut back the leading shoot to 1.5m (5ft) above the ground (*above*). Cut out close to the main stem all lateral shoots within 45cm (18in) of the ground. This then leaves the lateral shoots that will form the tree's main branches and framework. Prune back each of these shoots by half, cutting to a downward-pointing bud. This framework will eventually form a pyramid 1.8–2.1m (6–7ft) high and about 1.2m (4ft) wide, which can be accommodated in many gardens and does not need a supporting framework of wires.

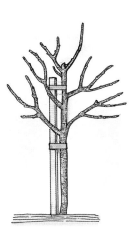

*3* During the latter part of mid-summer of the same year, use sharp secateurs to shorten the current season's growth to 20cm (8in) long and a downward-pointing bud. Also, cut back sideshoots to 15cm (6in) long. Do not prune the leading shoot.

## HALF-STANDARD PLUM TREES

**This is a popular way to grow plums and gages, where they are trained to form trunks 1.3m (4½ ft) long – Full standard types have trunks 1.8m (6ft) long and are too large for most gardens. Plant a two-year-old tree in late autumn or early winter and secure the stem to an H-shaped framework.**

In early spring, as growth begins, cut back the stem to 1.3m (4½ ft) above the ground and shorten sideshoots to 7.5–10cm (3–4in) long.

During the following early spring, choose three or four well-spaced branches and use sharp secateurs to cut them back by half. Completely remove any others.

In the next spring, shorten by about half the shoots that make up the main framework. In later years, just cut out any dead and crossing branches.

*4* In early spring, prune the central shoot by about two-thirds of the growth produced during the previous summer. Repeat this in the following spring until the stem has reached the desired height. Thereafter, cut back the leading shoot by 2.5cm (1in).

*5* During the latter part of mid-summer of the same year, shorten the current season's growth on each of the leading shoots to eight leaves from its point of origin. Prune back lateral shoots to leave six leaves. Cut out vigorous shoots growing at the top of the tree.

# PEACHES AND NECTARINES
## *Bushes*

These two succulent fruits are closely related, and both are cousins of the almond. Nectarines are simply smooth-skinned forms of the peach, slightly smaller and often considered to have a better, sweeter flavour. They respond to the same growing and pruning techniques, but nectarines are slightly less hardy than peaches. As well as being grown as bushes, these fruits are frequently grown as fans against a warm wall (*see pages 90 and 91*). The yield of fruit varies widely and much depends on the weather and the size of the tree.

Peaches and nectarines bear fruits on shoots produced during the previous season. Therefore, it is essential throughout each year of the bush's life to encourage the development of new shoots to replace those that have borne fruits. There are three distinctive types of buds on peaches and nectarines: fruit buds that are plump and develop fruits; growth buds that are pointed and produce shoots; triple buds are more complicated, having a central fruit bud which is plump, with growth buds on either side. Clearly, it is essential to prune shoots back to a growth bud when the development of a young shoot is desired. However, if a growth bud is not present, prune back to a triple bud.

### ALMONDS

The sweet almond (*Prunus dulcis*) can be grown as a bush in exactly the same way as peaches and nectarines. The bush grows 4.5–6m (15–20ft) high and wide and needs a large garden. Its nuts appear three or four years after the bush is planted and are borne on one-year-old wood, so each year it is essential to ensure the continuous production of fresh, healthy shoots.

Almonds need warm, dry summers with frost-free winters and in temperate climates they can only be grown successfully in the warmest regions. The nuts are harvested when their hulls (outer casings) start to crack.

The almond is thought to be native to the Near East. It is widely grown commercially in California, Australia and South Africa.

**Bush training**

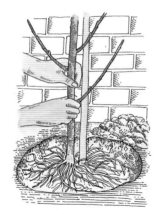

*1* From late autumn to mid-winter, plant two-year-old bush peaches, nectarines and almonds. Stake the tree and firm soil over the roots. As a bush, the tree will spread 3.6–4.5m (12–15ft) wide, so although it benefits from the protection of a wall, do not plant it too close. Late spring frosts and cold winds can be very damaging.

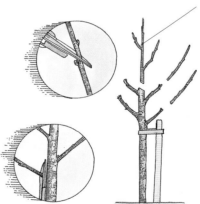

*2* In early spring of the following year, when the buds start to grow, cut back the leading shoot to 75–90cm (2½–3ft) high and slightly above a strong lateral shoot. The head is formed of three or four lateral shoots; cut each back by two-thirds to an outward-facing bud. Cut off all other laterals close to the main stem. The purpose of this

Cut back the central stem to a strong lateral shoot, 75–90cm (2½–3ft) above the ground.

Cut back the main laterals by two-thirds and to an outward-facing bud.

initial pruning is to form a head of well-spaced branches. Ensure that selected laterals are strong and healthy because if, at a later date, one has to be removed it will upset the bush's balance. Also at this time, check that the stem is well-secured to a stake – but not constricted. There are several types of adjustable 'plastic' tree-ties available.

Use sharp secateurs to cut off shoots growing from the main stem and below the bush's head.

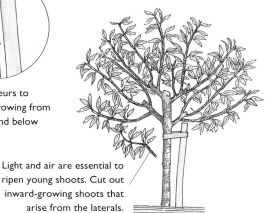

Light and air are essential to ripen young shoots. Cut out inward-growing shoots that arise from the laterals.

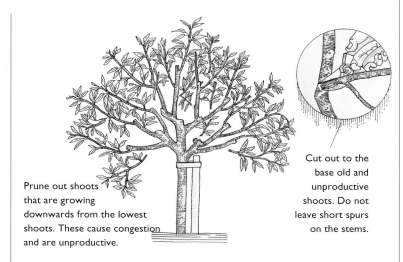

Prune out shoots that are growing downwards from the lowest shoots. These cause congestion and are unproductive.

Cut out to the base old and unproductive shoots. Do not leave short spurs on the stems.

3 During the subsequent summer, young shoots will develop from the four main laterals that were cut back in early spring. Do not prune these during summer. However, cut out to their bases shoots that are growing from them and towards the bush's centre. If left, they cause congestion. Additionally, cut off, flush with the main stem, shoots that are growing below the main framework.

5 By early to mid-summer of the following year, the tree will be clothed in leaves and shoots that have developed from the cut-back shoots. Cut to their bases old shoots, those that cross the bush's centre as well as those that cause congestion and prevent the circulation or air and entry of light. During summer, carefully use sharp secateurs to remove a few of the shoots that have borne fruits.

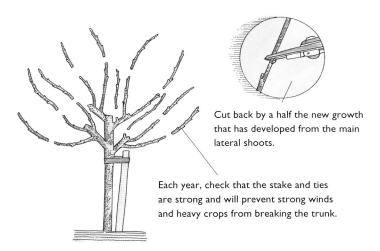

Cut back by a half the new growth that has developed from the main lateral shoots.

Each year, check that the stake and ties are strong and will prevent strong winds and heavy crops from breaking the trunk.

4 In early spring of the following year, cut back the young shoots – those that developed from shoots that were cut back during the previous spring – by half. Sever them just above a healthy, outward-facing bud. Cutting back shoots in this way ensures the development of a strong framework of branches. Cut back sub-laterals to about 10cm (4in) from their bases. Additionally, cut out shoots that cross and crowd the bush's centre, as well as those that rub against each other and might subsequently cause damage through which diseases could enter the bush. As the bush develops, the aim must be to ensure it has an open centre and that young branches are allowed to develop to replace those that are pulled down each year under the weight of fruit and have therefore to be cut out.

## THINNING CONGESTED FRUIT

During the first year, remove all blossom to ensure that the plant's energies are totally directed towards developing a strong framework. In the second year, leave the blossom intact but allow only a few fruits to mature. In all subsequent years, the fruits must be thinned. This is especially important when peaches and nectarines are being grown on fan-trained trees against a wall. This is performed from early to mid-summer. If this is neglected, the fruits do not grow to their full size. Also, they are congested and rub against each other.

LEFT Start thinning the fruits when they are the size of large peas and stop when they reach the size of walnuts. First, reduce the pea-sized fruits to singles, eventually spacing peaches 23cm (9in) apart and nectarines 15cm (6in). When grown on bushes they can be left slightly closer.

# PEACHES AND NECTARINES
## *Fan Trained*

Peaches and nectarines, as well as apricots (*see below*) can be grown as fan-trained trees against warm, sunny walls. These fruits can also be grown against a wooden fence, but as the lifespan of the fan is often more than that of a wooden fence, a brick wall is always a better choice. The objective with a fan-trained tree is to cover the space with branches that radiate from the tree's base, so that each branch receives the maximum amount of light and air. Building up the fan's framework is a long task and cannot be rushed. It is essential to create the fan from the base upwards, so that the central area is the last part to be filled.

Unlike many apple varieties, which have a long storage life, peaches and nectarines will keep only for about a week after being picked. It is often wiser to grow a fan-trained tree that requires very little garden space and produces only 13.5kg (30lb) of fruit than a bush form that can yield up to three times this amount and takes up vastly more room. A bush peach or nectarine is easier to grow than a fan-trained tree, but there is little point in producing a large crop of fruits if there are too many to eat within the time they can be stored after being harvested. Additionally, fan-trained trees are often more interesting to grow than a bush type.

---

### PRUNING APRICOTS

This popular fruit ripens from mid-summer to early autumn, depending on the variety and area. The formation of a fan-trained apricot tree is, initially, the same as that required for fan-trained peaches and nectarines (RIGHT). But once established, they need to be pruned in the same way recommended for fan-trained plums. This is because apricots bear most of their fruits on short spurs of two- and three-year-old wood. Because there is not such a need to replenish fruited shoots yearly with young ones (as in the case of peaches and nectarines), pruning is less demanding. Instead, every four to six years cut out old shoots which have borne fruits to enable young ones to develop and replace them. Tie in new shoots, but do not begin to prune them until they reach their second season.

When growing bush apricots, the initial pruning they need is the same as that performed for bush plums see pages 86 and 87, but prune them in early spring as soon as growth resumes. Later pruning of bush apricots is done in the same way as acid cherries when grown as bushes see page 93.

---

**Creating a fan-trained tree**

 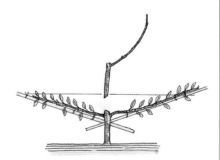

1 When creating a fan-trained peach or nectarine tree, plant a two-year-old tree (or feathered maiden) between late autumn and mid-winter. Position it about 20cm (8in) from a wall. In late winter, cut back the main stem to about 60cm (2ft) above the ground and slightly above a strong lateral. Also cut back all other laterals to one bud from their bases. In early summer (*above*), a few shoots will have formed: remove all but the top one and two others, lower down and preferably opposite each other.

2 A few months later, in the latter part of mid-summer, use sharp secateurs to cut off the central stem and then tie the two arms at the plant's base to individual canes. These canes are tied to the supporting wires, with the stems loosely but securely tied to them. After the central stem has been cut out, use a fungicidal paint to coat the surface to prevent diseases entering the plant. It is vital to create the base of a fan before building up its centre. If one arm of the fan is not growing strongly, do not lower it initially as far as the other one.

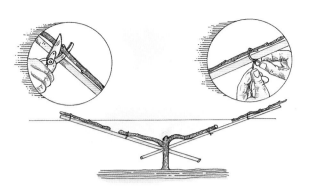

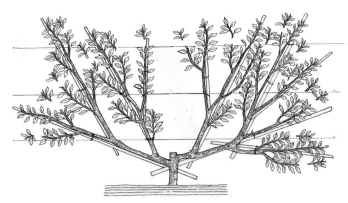

*3* In early spring of the following year, just when growth is beginning, cut back the two arms to a growth bud (sometimes known as a wood bud and identified as small and pointed) or a triple bud (two growth buds either side of a fruiting bud). Cut the stems 30–45cm (12–18in) from the main central stem (*above*).

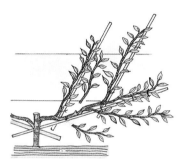

*4* During late spring and summer, young shoots will develop from buds at the ends of the cut-back arms, as well as along it. Select four strong shoots – two on the upper side and two on the lower part – on each of the arms (*above*). Cut off all other sideshoots but leave one leaf at the base of each one. For each of these eight shoots – four on either side – tie a strong bamboo cane to the tiers of wires, then secure the shoot to it. Spread out the canes so that the shoots are equally spaced but leaving a wide gap at the fan's centre. This later becomes filled.

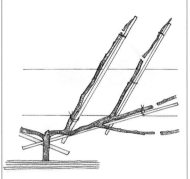

*5* In early spring of the following year, cut back the new growth on each of these eight shoots by about a third. Make these cuts slightly above a downward-pointing growth bud.

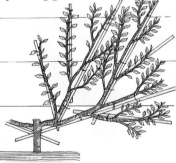

*6* During summer, let the ends of the shoots grow naturally (*above*). Allow three new shoots to develop on each of the arms; tie them to canes and then to the wires. Space them equally. Rub out buds growing towards the wall. Allow shoots to grow every 10cm (4in) along the upper and lower sides of the ribs.

*7* In late summer, after the lateral shoots that were selected earlier in the year are 45cm (18in) long, nip out their growing points. These are the young shoots that will bear fruit during the following year. Each year it is essential to encourage the development of fresh shoots that will bear fruits. If this is neglected, the yearly crop rapidly diminishes.

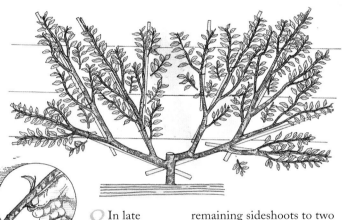

*8* In late spring and early summer of the same and all subsequent years, completely remove shoots which are growing towards and away from the wall. If they have flower buds at their bases, cut them to two leaves long. Young shoots produced during the previous year will bear fruits during the current season and should be bearing blossom and young sideshoots by early summer. At the base of each of these shoots, choose one sideshoot (to form a later replacement shoot), another in the middle (to act as a reserve shoot) and one at the tip to extend the fruit-bearing lateral. Pinch back the remaining sideshoots to two leaves from their bases. Later, when the replacement shoot at the base, as well as the reserve shoot, are 45cm (18in) long, and the extension shoot has formed six leaves, nip out the growing points of each of them. When the fruits have been picked, cut back each fruited lateral to the replacement shoot at its base. Should this shoot be damaged or not sufficiently vigorous, cut back to the reserve replacement shoot.

During the following year and subsequent years, repeat this process, always trying to encourage the development of fresh shoots that will bear fruit during the following year.

# CHERRIES *Fan trained*

Sweet and acid cherries are popular summer fruits; to many people they are the epitome of a country garden. Sweet cherries are more vigorous than the acid variety and are therefore best reserved for large gardens or orchards. Acid cherries are better suited to small gardens. Sweet cherries are derived from *Prunus avium*, with white flowers in spring and fruits ranging in colour from yellow and pink to black during the latter part of early summer until mid-summer. Varieties to consider include 'Early Rivers' (deep red flesh), 'Governor Wood' (dark red with yellow flesh), 'Merton Bigarreau' (black) and 'Van' (red). Acid cherries are derived from *Prunus cerasus*, with fruits that ripen from mid- to late summer. The fruits are tart, however, and when eaten raw are not to everyone's taste. Varieties to consider include 'Morello' (dark red) and 'Kentish Red' (scarlet, with yellow flesh).

## SWEET AND DUKE CHERRIES

Sweet cherries, also known as dessert cherries, are a favourite fruit and ready for picking about mid-summer. They are derived from *Prunus avium*. The Duke Cherry is a cross between the sweet and acid types but is pruned in the same way as the sweet ones.

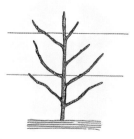

*1* Plant a bare-rooted two-year-old tree (feathered maiden) during its dormant period, from late autumn to early spring. Container-grown trees can be planted at any time when the soil is neither frozen nor water-logged. Plant the tree alongside tiered wires, spaced about 23cm (9in) apart, from 30cm (12in) above the ground to about 2.1m (7ft) high.

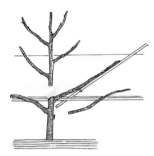

*2* During the following spring, select two strong sideshoots near the base and use sharp secateurs to cut off the central stem, just above the top one. Tie the sideshoots to two canes, then to the wires.

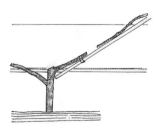

*3* In spring of the following year, cut each lateral shoot to about 30cm (12in) from the central stem. Cut them slightly above an outward-pointing bud. This severe pruning encourages the development of a strong framework.

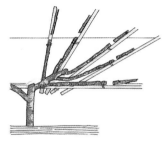

*4* During summer, shoots grow from the two arms. Tie them to canes and train into position. In the spring, cut them back to outward-pointing buds, leaving 45–50cm (18–20in) of new growth.

*5* In the following spring and subsequent ones, rub out young shoots that are growing outwards or directly towards the wall. This is also a way to ensure that shoots are equally spaced.

### PICKING CHERRIES

Leave the fruits on the tree until they are fully ripe. If, however, they start cracking, pick them immediately. Sweet cherries can be eaten raw, while acid types have culinary qualities. If the fruits are to be frozen, pick them while still firm. When picking the fruits, use sharp scissors to cut each stalk close to the shoot. If the cherry stalks are pulled off, the bark may be damaged, which can encourage the entry of diseases such as bacterial canker. Place the picked fruits in a basket, taking care not to bruise them.

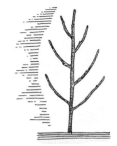

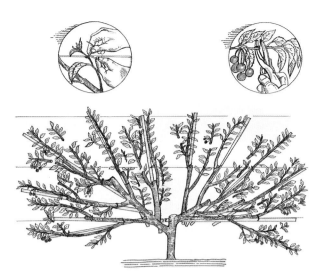

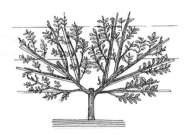

**6** In the latter part of mid-summer of the same year, cut back to five or six leaves all shoots that are not needed to extend or build up the framework. Also tie in sideshoots that are required to fill up bare areas or to replace old wood. Eventually, shoots will reach the top of the wall; then cut them back to a weak lateral shoot.

**ACID CHERRIES**

These have a different heritage from the sweet types and the fruits are smaller. They are less vigorous and often known as sour cherries. Because of the tartness of the fruits they are not often eaten raw. Instead, they are used in preserves and for other culinary purposes. Unlike the sweet cherries, which bear fruits on spurs on two-year-old and older wood, acid cherries develop most of their fruits on one-year-old shoots produced during the previous year. Therefore there is a need to ensure that fresh shoots are produced each year to replace those that have fruited and been cut out.

With acid cherries the aim is to restrict excessive vegetative growth and to encourage the formation of fruit buds.

Cherries have been popular for many centuries: cherry orchards were known in England in the 1500s, while in 1833 an American fruit book notes nearly fifty varieties.

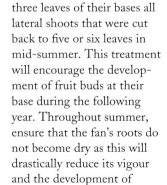

**7** By the end of early autumn, the shoots will have grown further but their growth will be slowing down. Use sharp secateurs to cut back to three leaves of their bases all lateral shoots that were cut back to five or six leaves in mid-summer. This treatment will encourage the development of fruit buds at their base during the following year. Throughout summer, ensure that the fan's roots do not become dry as this will drastically reduce its vigour and the development of young, healthy, new shoots.

**1** The pruning of a fan-trained acid cherry for the first three years is exactly the same as recommended for fan-trained peach trees (*see pages 90 and 91*). This encompasses the planting, initial pruning and the first three years of growth encouraging the build-up of the fan's framework, with equally-spaced ribs. During the third year, allow the leading shoots on each rib to create extension growth. Tie these shoots to strong canes which are firmly secured to the wires.

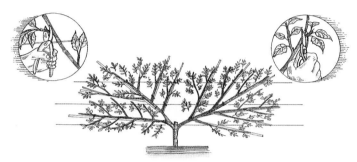

**2** In late spring of the fourth and subsequent years, thin out new shoots to 10–15cm (4–6in) apart and tie them to the wires while they are still flexible. Leave a replacement shoot at the base of each lateral that will bear fruit. Cut out at their base all shoots that point directly at the wall. Allow the ends of the young shoots to grow naturally, where there is room, to clothe the wall with growth.

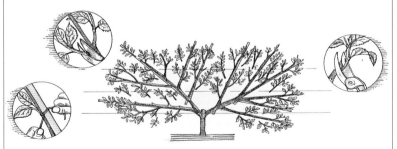

**3** After the fan has borne fruits during the fourth year and subsequent years, cut out lateral shoots that have borne fruit to the young replacement shoot that was left when pruning during spring. Cut out shoots that have developed during summer and are pointing either towards the wall or directly away from it. Inspect all shoots to ensure they are tied to the canes and wires. It is essential that the shoots are not able to be blown about by the wind.

# FIGS, ELDERBERRIES AND MULBERRIES

These are popular but seldom-grown fruits that deserve greater publicity. In earlier times, however, they were well known; the Romans are said to have planted figs throughout Europe two thousand years ago. Figs, elderberries and mulberries were also widely featured in North American fruit books at the beginning of the 1800s. Much of the fame of figs lies with their succulent fruits, which can be eaten fresh or dried. The leaves were used in the East in the past for the preservation of embalmed bodies, while a boiling down of green branches and leaves produced a deep golden dye. The leaves on their own produced a deep yellow stain, with a fragrance that remained in the cloth even after several washings. The fruits are also used to make a well-known laxative. The black mulberry also has a medicinal value, forming a syrup to soothe sore throats. Elderberry wine is known in Europe and North America, while in Germany a strong spirit was distilled from the fruit.

**Fan-trained fig**

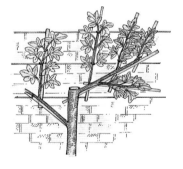

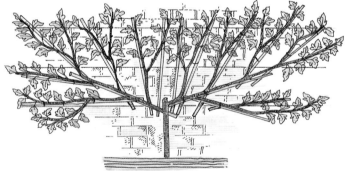

*1* To form a fan-trained fig tree, in winter plant a two-year-old container-grown specimen in the shelter of a warm wall but 15–20cm (6–8in) away from its base. Remove the container and position the plant about 10cm (4in) deeper than before. Erect supporting wires, 23cm (9in) apart, from 45cm (18in) above the ground to the top of the wall. In spring, cut back the central stem to just above the lowest wire and immediately above a lateral shoot. Select two shoots to form the arms and tie them to canes secured at 45 degrees to the wires. Cut back both arms to a bud 45cm (18in) from the trunk. Cut off other laterals.

*2* During the following summer, allow four shoots to grow from each of the two arms – one at the end of the arm to form extension growth, one from the underside and two on the top side. Rub out all other buds growing from the arms and secure the eight shoots to bamboo canes. The objective at this stage is to form a strong framework of branches that are spaced out so that light and air can enter the fan. Allow plenty of space between the newly formed ribs, as fig leaves are large and create a great deal of shade.

*3* In late winter of the following year, prune back each of the main shoots, cutting slightly above a bud which will continue its growth in the desired direction; leave about 60cm (2ft) of the previous season's growth. During summer, allow further shoots to develop. Rub out unwanted buds. It takes several years to create a framework.

## RESTRICTING FIG ROOTS

The roots of figs must be constrained to prevent them producing masses of leafy growth and few fruits. Prepare the planting area by digging a hole 60cm (2ft) square and deep. Line it with bricks or paving slabs and fill with 30cm (12in) of rubble. Then fill with soil with rubble added.

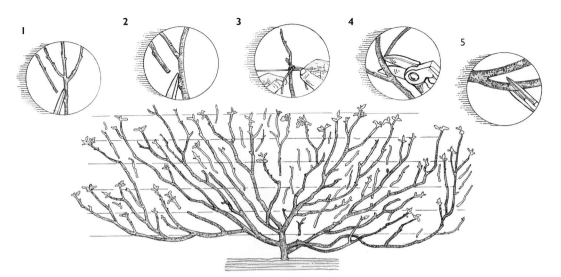

4 It often takes four years to create a framework of evenly spaced ribs on the fan. Once this has been achieved, the routine is to prune the fan in spring and again in summer. In spring, use sharp secateurs to cut out diseased and frost-damaged shoots (1); thin out young shoots to just above one bud from their base (2); position and tie in young shoots (3); completely remove shoots growing towards and away from the wall (4); and cut out some of the old, bare shoots to slightly above the first bud from its base (5). Later in the year, during early summer, cut back young growths to five leaves from their base. These will promote fruiting shoots for the following year.

LEFT The black mulberry tree is ornamental and also famed for its juicy, dark-red fruits that resemble those of the loganberry. The berries are best when eaten fresh, and they introduce a distinctively sharp flavour to jams and wines. The juice is bright purplish-red and, when eating the fruits, hands and lips often become strongly stained.

## ELDERBERRIES

The fruits of the common elder (*Sambucus nigra*) are frequently fermented to make elderberry wine. In North America it is the sweet elder (*S. canadensis*) that is mainly used. After planting bare-rooted plants in winter, prune back healthy shoots to outward-facing buds. Completely cut out thin, diseased and crossing shoots. In winter cut out some old shoots at ground level to encourage the development of new ones and cut out dead and diseased shoots.

## FIGS

This fruit has been grown since early times and, although best in subtropical regions, it thrives in warm areas in temperate countries. The fruits are borne on the tips of well-ripened shoots produced during the previous summer. Second crops are sometimes developed on shoots produced earlier in the year, but these seldom ripen in temperate lands and are best removed in early autumn. In cool regions, fan-trained trees against a warm, sheltered wall are better than bushes.

Fruits ripen between late summer and mid-autumn, and as the stalk softens they hang down. If figs become too rampant, their growth can be controlled by root-pruning.

## MULBERRIES

The common or black mulberry (*Morus nigra*) probably comes from Asia but has for many years been established in Europe and North America. The juicy fruits are picked as soon as they are ripe in late summer. It forms a large, slow-growing tree and takes about eight years to bear fruits. Little pruning is needed; indeed, cuts are likely to bleed and must be cauterized with a hot poker. When young, in winter and fully dormant, prune only to establish a strong framework of four or five branches. Afterwards, prune to remove dead or misplaced branches – and only in winter.

The white mulberry (*M. alba*) has sweet but insipid, white, pink or purplish fruits, and is mainly grown for its light-green leaves, so beloved by silkworms.

# RED AND WHITE CURRANTS

Red currants and white currants are pruned in the same way, but quite differently from blackcurrants. Instead of forming 'stools' in the manner of blackcurrants, with new shoots developing from ground level or from previously pruned stems close to the plant's base, red and white currants grow on bushes with 'legs'. These are stems 15–20cm (6–8in) long that connect the roots with the branches. The branches should not arise from soil level.

Red and white currants produce fruits on short spurs which develop on the old wood, as well as in clusters at the base of young growths formed during the previous year. Like many other fruits, they need to be pruned in both winter and summer, especially when trained as cordons. Summer-pruning helps to create fruiting spurs without encouraging the growth of shoots. Bush-grown types yield 3.5–4.5kg (8–10lb) of fruit, while single cordons in the region of 1–1.3kg (2–3lb).

**Bush-grown red and white currants**

 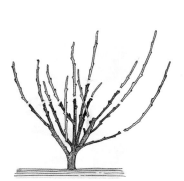  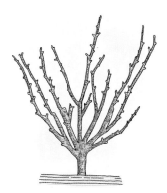

*1* Plant both red and white currants during their dormant period, from late autumn to late winter, using a one-year-old plant (*above*). Plant the bush slightly lower than it was positioned before. During winter, prune back all shoots by half, cutting to just above an outward-pointing bud (*below*).

*2* During the second dormant period, when the bush is two years old, prune each branch back by half to an outward-pointing bud. In the third year (*above*), cut all leading shoots back by 15cm (6in) during their dormant period. Always cut the shoots to just above an outward-pointing bud. Cut back lateral shoots to about two buds from their bases. Every winter during the first few years, check that the soil is firm around the roots and has not been lifted by the action of frost.

Occasionally, two-year-old bushes are planted, and this reduces the initial time taken to produce fruit.

*3* During the fourth and subsequent years, it is only necessary to cut back the leading shoots by 2.5cm (1in), or even less. Continue to cut back lateral shoots to form new spurs, and to remove old shoots from the plant's centre. Each year – about the end of early summer – cut back new lateral shoots to about five leaves from their bases. Do not prune the leading shoots. Use sharp secateurs.

ABOVE Red currants are hardy deciduous shrubs grown in temperate areas. They are ideal summer fruits for small gardens.

## STANDARD RED CURRANTS

Growing red currants to form heads about 1.2m (4ft) high is an unusual but not difficult way to grow this fruit. During winter, take hardwood cuttings about 38cm (15in) long, remove all buds from the lower 15cm (6in) and insert them about 13cm (5in) into sandy, well-drained soil. When a year old, move it to its growing position, tie the leading shoot to a stake and pinch all sideshoots back to two leaves. As they develop, cut back to one leaf all shoots that develop from the pinched-back sideshoots. Continue this technique until the leading shoot reaches about 1.2m (4ft) high, then in autumn cut it back by about 10cm (4in) to a healthy bud. During the following spring, select three or four shoots near to the stem's top that will form the head. Do not pinch them back, but in autumn prune them to 10–15cm (4–6in) from their base. By the following autumn, shoots will have developed from this framework and these are cut back to 15cm (6in) from their base. The formation of a strong head is essential.

Once the head is formed, pruning involves cutting back in autumn all sideshoots to two buds from their base. The left-hand side of the standard illustrated here has been pruned, the right side unpruned. In addition, cut back leading shoots to 15cm (6in) long if weak, but 20–23cm (8–9in) if strong.

During the standard's third year, gradually cut away all the shoots from its stem.

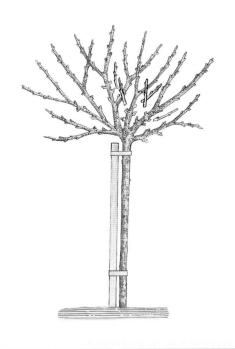

**Cordon red and white currants**

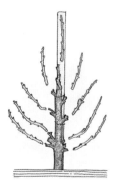

*1* Plant one-year-old cordon red and white currants during winter, setting them 38cm (15in) apart. At this stage, each plant will have a central stem and about four sideshoots. Immediately, shorten the central shoot by a third to a half of its length, cutting to an outward-facing bud. Cut back lateral shoots to one bud from their base, but completely remove those within 10cm (4in) of the ground. Stake each plant.

*3* During the second and later years, prune cordons in winter; cut back the leading shoot to slightly above a healthy bud and remove all but 15cm (6in) of the new growth. In later years cut back the leading shoot to leave only one bud of new growth. Also, cut back to leave 2.5cm (1in) of new growth on all lateral shoots that were pruned during the previous summer. Pick up and burn any wood cut from the plants.

*2* In the following year, during the early part of mid-summer, prune back the current season's sideshoots to four or five leaves from their base. Do not prune the leading shoot at this stage, but ensure the new growth – as well as the previous season's wood – is tied to the supporting stake. Ensure that these ties do not strangle the shoots: first, securely tie the string to the stake, then loop it around a stem.

*4* During the following summer – and all subsequent ones – leave pruning the leading shoot until winter, but cut back the sideshoots to leave four or five leaves of fresh growth produced earlier during the same season. Continue to tie the central, leading shoot to a support, but remember that during the following winter it will be cut back to leave only one bud of fresh growth.

# BLACKCURRANTS

Blackcurrants are easily grown and pruned. They can be planted at any time during their dormant period, from mid-autumn to early spring, and eventually form large bushes with stems growing from soil level. Plants grown in this way – with new growth produced from ground level – are known as stools. Blackcurrants produce their best fruit on shoots that developed during the previous season, although some fruits are borne on older wood. The yearly cycle of pruning is designed to cut out much of the older wood that has borne fruit and to encourage the development of young shoots. Pruning in this way also helps to prevent the bush becoming congested with shoots.

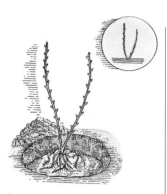

*1* Plant young blackcurrant bushes during their dormant period, setting them slightly deeper than before – the old soil level mark can be seen on the stem.

*2* Firm soil around and over the roots, then immediately cut back all stems to about 2.5cm (1in) above soil level. Although this may appear to be drastic, it encourages the development of fresh, young shoots from the plant's base during the following year. If this initial pruning is neglected, the quality and amount of fruit will be radically diminished.

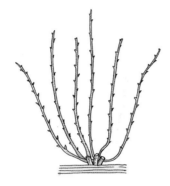

*3* By the end of the following summer, young shoots will have developed and by autumn, when their leaves have fallen off, will resemble the above plant. No pruning is needed at this stage. During the following year, these stems will bear fruit (*below*). At the same time, fresh shoots will have developed from the bush's base and these, too, will later bear fruits.

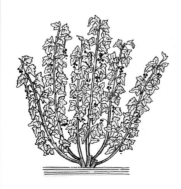

*4* During all subsequent years, prune the bush preferably as soon as the fruit has been picked, but autumn is also suitable. First, cut out old wood to its base. This will remove the majority of shoots that produced fruit during the current season. Cut out damaged and crossing shoots so that light and air can penetrate the bush to assist in the ripening of young shoots.

## REJUVENATING OLD BUSHES

When blackcurrant bushes are neglected they become a mass of old shoots that bear few and inferior fruits. If the bushes are especially old and full of dark wood, they are best pulled out and replanted with fresh, young plants. But if the neglect has been for only three or four years, they can be rejuvenated by cutting all stems to their bases in late summer or early autumn. Drastic pruning such as this encourages the development of new shoots from ground level and the plant's base. However, it does mean that no fruit will be produced during the following year, when a mass of one-year-old shoots will be created.

To encourage the development of these young stems after cutting back in spring sprinkle a general fertilizer around the bush, water thoroughly and then add a mulch. Also, during summer keep the soil moist and pull up any weeds growing around the plant's base.

# GOOSEBERRIES

Unlike blackcurrants, which form a mass of stems from ground level, gooseberries develop a short stem known as a 'leg', which supports the branches on which the fruits are borne. Most gooseberries are grown as bushes, but some can be trained as single, double or even triple cordons, as well as in fan shapes. Gooseberry bushes – and other trained forms – bear fruits on one-year-old wood and spurs that develop from older shoots. With cordon gooseberries, fruits are borne on spurs that develop directly from the plant's main stem and create an unusual and attractive feature.

The initial pruning of bushes is directed to creating a strong framework of permanent branches, evenly spaced around the main stem. Later pruning for both bushes and specially trained forms involves cutting them in both winter and summer.

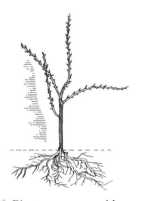

1 Plant a one-year-old (maiden) gooseberry bush during its dormant period, from late autumn to late winter. Set the plant firmly in the soil, only fractionally deeper than before, ensuring it has a 'leg'.

3 By late autumn or early winter of the following year, strong shoots will have developed from the cut-back stems. Shorten them back by a half to inward- and upward-pointing buds. By the following late autumn (*right*), further growth will have developed; shorten all leading shoots by a half. Shorten laterals to 5cm (2in) long and cut out crossing shoots.

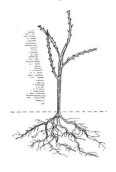

2 Immediately prune back each main branch by a half, cutting to an upward-pointing bud. Ensure that the plant has a stem 15–20cm (6–8in) long.

4 In all subsequent years, during the latter part of early summer, prune all lateral shoots produced that season to five leaves. Do not prune leader shoots. During the following winter, cut back leader shoots by half, and all lateral shoots to about two buds from their base; before and after (*below*).

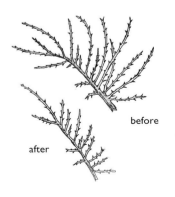

before

after

## THINNING GOOSEBERRIES

Dessert gooseberries are succulent. Their size can be increased by thinning them in early summer, removing every other fruit. These can then be used in pies and for bottling. The remaining berries swell and develop into very juicy fruits. During the middle of the nineteenth century, growing large berries was a popular pastime. Individual berries in excess of 50g (nearly 2oz) were often grown. In earlier centuries, gooseberries were a popular cottage garden fruit – the name comes from a sauce in which they were cooked and which was eaten with a succulent and tasty goose.

# RASPBERRIES

Summer-fruiting raspberries are, after strawberries, the most popular and widely grown soft fruit and to many people they are the epitome of summer fruits; even the bouquet of freshly picked fruits excites the taste buds! Yields of 2–3kg (5–6lb) for each 90cm (36in) of row of summer-fruiting varieties can be expected, and 200g (½ lb) is about right for autumn-fruiting types. By having both summer- and autumn-fruiting raspberries it is possible to have fresh fruits from mid-summer through to the frosts of autumn. They can be frozen if there is a long gap between harvesting the summer and autumn types.

Summer-fruiting varieties to consider include: 'Glen Cova' (early; abundant and well-flavoured), 'Glen Moy' (early; well-flavoured fruits on spine-free canes), 'Leo' (late; medium-sized fruits with a good flavour), 'Malling Admiral' (mid-season; heavy cropper with well-flavoured fruits) and 'Malling Jewel' (mid-season; good crops, but often produces only a few canes). There are also yellow-fruiting varieties.

Autumn-fruiting varieties to consider include: 'Heritage' (medium-sized fruits, but only suitable for mild areas), 'Zeva' (large berries, but handle carefully as they tend to crumble) and 'Fallgold' (sweet, yellow, medium-sized fruits).

**PICKING RASPBERRIES**

Pick raspberries as soon as they are showing an even red colour (unless they are of the yellow varieties). Hold them gently but firmly and, with a bending and twisting action, remove individual fruits from the canes. The stalk and core (often known as the plug) should remain on the plant and not attached to the fruit. Put them in shallow layers, no more than 5cm (2in) deep, in containers and place in a cool, shaded area, so that they lose their 'field' heat. Raspberries are soon bruised and must be handled carefully.

When raspberries are grown for showing, use sharp scissors to remove them from the plant. Cut them with the core still attached. Fruits which are to be used for dessert – rather than for eating or freezing immediately – are often picked with their plugs still present, as it assists in keeping them fresh.

**Summer-fruiting raspberries**

*1* Plant summer-fruiting raspberry canes from late autumn to early spring, whenever the soil is not frozen or waterlogged. Plant the canes 45cm (18in) apart and about 7.5cm (3in) deep in well-prepared soil to which has been added compost or manure. Spread out the roots and firm soil over them. Too deep planting inhibits the development of new canes. Align the rows north to south to ensure one row does not excessively shade its neighbour, and if several rows are planted space them 1.8m (6ft) apart.

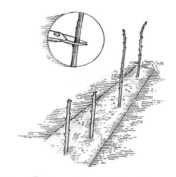

*2* Immediately after the canes are planted, cut them down to 23–30cm (9–12in) high and just above a healthy, dormant bud. While the canes are small is the time to erect tiers of strong supporting wires, 75cm (2½ft), 1m (3½ft) and 1.6m (5½ft) above the ground (for further details of this method and two others, *see page 103*). Whatever its construction, it must be strong and able to support the canes for six or more years. In late winter, re-firm soil around roots loosened by frost.

*3* In spring, young shoots that appear from ground level will bear fruits during the following year. At this stage, cut off the old, 23–30cm (9–12in) high cane, just above ground level. During the subsequent summer, space out these canes and tie them to the supporting wires. Do not allow more than eight canes to develop, although during the first year, when the plant is young, it is extremely unlikely that this number will form. During autumn, all the leaves fall off and only the bare canes are left.

4 In late winter, cut off the tips of all canes, about 15cm (6in) above the top wire (*right*). Use sharp secateurs to cut them slightly above a healthy bud. During the next summer, fresh canes will develop that produce fruits in the following year. In each spring, this cycle of canes produced during the previous year, and fresh shoots developing from the plant's base, is repeated.

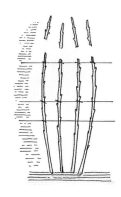

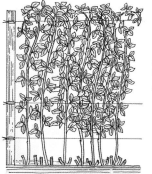

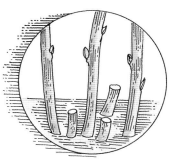

5 As soon as the fruits have been picked, cut down to their bases all canes that produced fruits. This will leave the young canes that developed earlier in the same year and which will produce fruits during the following season. Do not allow more than eight of these canes to develop from each plant. Space them out and tie to the wires, setting them about 10cm (4in) apart. If these young canes are strong and vigorous, also tie their tips to the top wire, forming a series of loops.

Tying the tops of canes in loops reduces the development of further vigorous growth. It also encourages both the tip of the cane and the rest of it to mature rapidly and to ripen. In cold and exposed areas, where the growing season is short, this assists the canes to survive without severe damage.

**Autumn-fruiting raspberries**

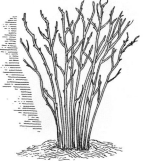

Autumn-fruiting raspberry canes are seldom attacked by birds and therefore do not need to be covered with netting.

1 Autumn-fruiting raspberries bear fruits on the tips of canes produced earlier during the same season. The fruits ripen from early autumn until the onset of frosts. The canes are best supported by the double-fence system (*see below*). Plant them in the same way as for the summer-fruiting types and allow the canes to develop: fruiting is usually sparse during the first year.

2 In late winter of each year, cut all of the canes to ground level. During spring, fresh shoots will develop which later will produce fruits in autumn. Train and guide the canes between the two tiers of wires. Cut out canes which are growing away from the row. Autumn-fruiting raspberries are easier to prune than summer ones, as all the canes are cut back at the same time.

## SUPPORTING CANES

**SINGLE-POST SYSTEM**
This is an easy way to support just a few canes in a small garden. Before planting the canes, knock 2.4m (8ft) long, 6cm (2½ in) thick poles 60cm (2ft) into the ground. The canes are later bunched around them and loosely tied with long loops of wire or strong string – they must not be held too tightly.

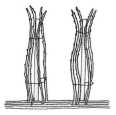

**SINGLE-FENCE SYSTEM**
This is the normal method of supporting raspberry canes. At either end of the row, put in place strong, 2.4m (8ft) long posts so that their tops are about 1.8m (6ft) above the ground. Then, stretch galvanized wires between them at 75cm (2½ft), 1m (3½ft) and 1.6m (5½ft) above the ground.

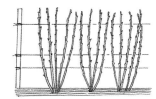

**DOUBLE-FENCE SYSTEM**
At each end of a row, drive a 2.1m (7ft) long, square-cut, 6cm (2½ in) thick, post into the ground so that its top is 1.5–1.6m (5–5½ft) high. Then, fix two 75cm (2½ft) long battens to the outer side of each post. Stretch strong, rust-resistant, galvanized wires between them, so that the plants are enclosed and supported.

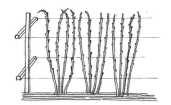

# BLACKBERRIES, HYBRID BERRIES AND LOGANBERRIES

The cultivated forms of blackberries are far plumper and sweeter than those gathered from hedgerows, and when established each plant yields 4.5–9kg (10–20lb) of fruit – sometimes 13.5kg (30lb). Varieties of blackberry include 'Bedford Giant' (vigorous, bright black fruits during mid- and late summer), 'Himalaya Giant' (medium-sized fruits during late summer) and 'Oregon Thornless' (a popular variety bearing thorn-free canes which fruits during late summer and into early autumn).

Hybrid berries have mainly evolved from crosses between blackberries and raspberries. They include Tayberries, Boysenberries and Dewberries. Most hybrid berries are not as vigorous as blackberries. Loganberries, another hybrid, are said to have originated in California from a natural cross between a raspberry and blackberry which was spotted by Judge J. H. Logan more than a century ago. The fruits are up to 5cm (2in) long, burgundy-red, with a sharp flavour and ready for picking during mid- and late summer. There are two clones: L654 (thornless) and LY59 (thorned).

ABOVE **A thornless loganberry tied to supporting wires.**

ABOVE **Blackberry 'Oregon Thornless' produces firm berries.**

**Weaving method**

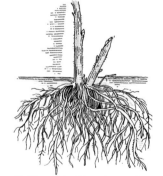

*1* Plant blackberries and hybrid berries at any time from mid-autumn to late winter, whenever the soil is not frozen or waterlogged. Position the young plants about 1.8–3m (6–10ft) apart against a series of tiered supporting wires. Vigorous varieties are better spaced 3.6m (12ft) apart. Each year the plants will produce young canes which, during the following season, bear fruits. It is therefore essential that the soil is fertile and retains moisture throughout summer and into early autumn.

*2* Immediately after being planted, cut down the stem to about 23cm (9in) above the ground, severing just above a healthy bud (*left*). This encourages the development of young shoots from ground level. In early spring, re-firm soil over the plant's roots; severe frosts often disturb the soil and, unless re-firmed, this retards a plant's subsequent growth. Use the heel of a shoe to firm the soil.

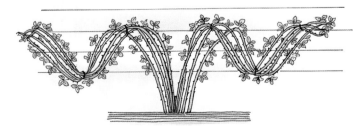

*3* During the first summer, young canes grow from the plant's base. Weave and secure them between the lower three tiers of wires, spreading them equally on both sides. At this stage, the top wire is left bare, so that young canes produced during the following year can be trained on them.

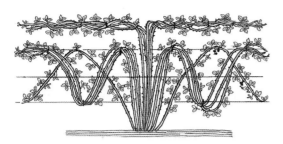

**4** During the following year, train in the new canes that developed from the plant's base, guiding them straight up and then in both directions along the top wire. Loosely tie them in clusters so that air and light can penetrate between them. The circulation of air helps to prevent the onset of diseases. Do not allow the two seasons' canes to become mixed as this will create problems later in the year.

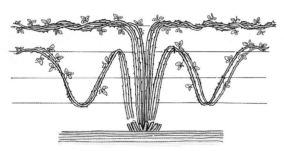

**5** In the latter part of mid-summer, the old canes start to bear fruits.

Immediately after fruiting is over, cut out to their bases all canes that produced fruits. Sever the ties that secure them to the wires and place them and the canes on a heap ready for burning. Never try to compost them. Wear stout gloves while pruning and freeing these old canes from their supporting wires.

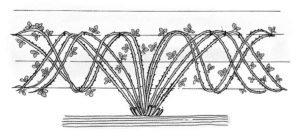

**6** When all the old canes have been removed, untie from the top wire all of those canes which were produced during the current year. These are the canes that will bear fruits during the following season. Light and air are essential at this stage to ripen the canes, so space them equally apart and not in clusters. In autumn, cut off the tips from weak and young canes. In late winter – and especially for plants growing in very cold and exposed areas – cut back the ends of shoots damaged by frost.

## FAN TRAINING

In addition to the weaving method – (detailed and illustrated LEFT) – there is the fan-trained system. It is ideal for blackberries, loganberries and other hybrid berries and, although it requires a great deal of attention, it produces a heavy crop. Sometimes, the new canes are grown in among the old ones, but a variation is to grow all the old canes on one side and the new ones on the other. This makes pruning easier as the old, fruited stems can be easily identified from the new ones. In the illustration (BELOW), the old canes are on the right side, the new ones on the left. Use soft string to tie the canes to the wires, loosely but securely.

## ROPING

This is an alternative system which involves tying the canes in groups of three or four to the wires. It is an easier and quicker system of training cane fruits than the fan method. By training the old and new canes on different sides of the plant, pruning is made easier. The illustration featured (BELOW) of the roping method shows the old, fruited canes which have just been cut off at their bases. During the following season, young canes will develop on the right side and these are arranged in small groups along the wires.

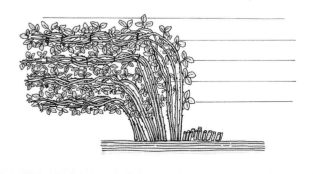

# BLUEBERRIES, CRANBERRIES AND KIWI FRUITS

Blueberries and cranberries are hardy shrubs that need acid soil to ensure their survival. The highbush blueberry (*Vaccinium corymbosum*) is native to North America and popular in blueberry pie, although the juicy fruits can also be eaten stewed with sugar. Cranberries (*V. accinium oxycoccos*) are also native to America, as well as Europe and the British Isles. Its fruits are used in cranberry sauce and served with turkey and venison. In addition, there are several related shrubby plants that yield edible berries, although they are infrequently grown in fruit gardens. These include bildberries (*V. myrtillus*, also known as bilberries, blaeberries and whortleberries), lowbush blueberries (*V. angustifolium*) and large or American cranberries (*V. marcrocarpon*).

The kiwi fruit is not so hardy. In a temperate region, this climber needs a warm climate or a sheltered position against a warm, sun-drenched wall.

**HIGHBUSH BLUEBERRY**

This is an ideal fruiting shrub in gardens with very acid soil, about pH 4.5. It so loves acid soil that it is likely to fail where the pH reading is above 5.5. For the first three years after planting, no pruning is needed. After this period the aim is to stimulate fresh growth which will bear fruit two years later: this is because blueberries bear fruit on the tips of the previous season's shoots.

BELOW In late summer, the ripening fruits of the blueberry are dark blue and covered in a greyish bloom. The plant's foliage is also attractive and turns a glowing red in autumn.

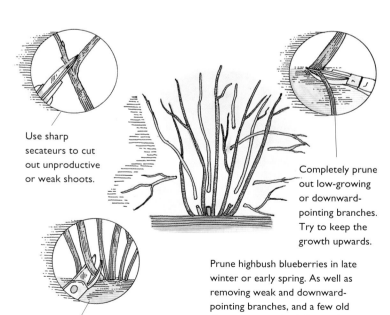

Use sharp secateurs to cut out unproductive or weak shoots.

Completely prune out low-growing or downward-pointing branches. Try to keep the growth upwards.

Prune highbush blueberries in late winter or early spring. As well as removing weak and downward-pointing branches, and a few old shoots, cut out dead shoots that may be congesting the bush's centre. If bushes are neglected and become crowded with old wood, completely cut out all but a few young shoots.

To encourage the development of fresh, fruit-bearing shoots, completely cut back a few of the oldest stems to their base.

## CRANBERRIES

This acid-loving plant is a close relative of the blueberry. It needs little pruning, other than occasionally cutting out very old stems in spring and ensuring it does not encroach upon neighbouring plants. To keep plants bushy, use hand shears in mid-spring to lightly clip off the ends of shoots. Rather than cutting off long shoots, they can be layered in autumn and encouraged to form roots. Sever rooted stems from the parent plant during the following autumn and re-plant them in spring.

BELOW Cranberry fruits are popular, bright red, rounded or broadly oval and grow on low, creeping, acid-loving bushes.

## KIWI FRUITS

These succulent fruits are native to China and also known as Chinese gooseberries. In New Zealand, where they are grown commercially, they are better known as kiwi fruits and kiwi berries, and in North America and China as yang-tao. They are borne on the climber *Actinidia chinensis*, widely grown in temperate climates for its large leaves SEE CLIMBERS ON PAGE 40. In temperate regions, low temperatures and late spring frosts make growing this climber for its fruits difficult, but in warm areas and against a warm wall it is possible.

### VARIETIES

The range of varieties for temperate areas is limited, but the best choice is 'Hayward'. It is late-flowering, with large, succulently flavoured fruits. In some catalogues it is listed as *Actinidia deliciosa* 'Hayward'.

### SEPARATE SEXES

As male and female flowers are borne on separate plants it is necessary to plant one of each for the production of fruits. Plants do not bear flowers for at least the first three years, and the fruits are usually smaller than those which are imported from warm climates. Plant young specimens in spring, putting male and female plants next to each other so that they are practically entwined. Grow them as espaliers. Cut each stem level with the bottom supporting wire immediately after planting. Allow two shoots to develop on each plant: one to grow vertically, the other to form an arm of the espalier. Repeat this training at each level of the espalier. Rub off unwanted buds growing on the main, vertical stems and between the horizontal arms. During late summer, pinch out the tips of the horizontal arms as well as shoots arising from them; this will encourage the development of fruiting spurs.

Male and female plants grown next to one another.

Kiwi fruits are best grown against a warm wall.

# GLOSSARY

**bark-ringing** The removal of a narrow strip of bark from a trunk to deter the production of vegetative growth and to encourage the development of fruits.

**biennial bearing** The tendency of some apple varieties to produce more fruit one year than during the following season.

**bleeding** The loss of sap from a plant through a cut. If pruning is performed at the wrong time, some plants freely exude sap.

**blossom bud** Also known as a fruit bud. It is much fatter than a vegetative bud.

**bole** A term for the trunk of a tree, from ground level to the lowest branch.

**bonsai** A technique used to enable trees and shrubs to remain small and to be grown in shallow containers. Traditional bonsai is essentially an outdoor technique, with specimens being taken indoors for only a day or so. A variation known as Chinese or indoor bonsai is now used to dwarf

tropical and subtropical shrubs that can be grown indoors throughout the year. Dwarfing is maintained by pruning roots, stems and leaves.

**breastwood** Shoots which grow outwards from woody plants trained against walls, trellises and other supporting structures.

**bush** Refers to trees where there is only a short trunk between the ground and the lowest branch, as well as to soft fruits such as blackcurrants which have a mass of stems at ground level. Gooseberries and both red and white currants are soft fruits which have a short stem between the roots and the shoots.

**callus** Hard, protective tissue which forms over a cut or wounded surface.

**central leader** The central, vertical and dominant stem on a tree.

**conifer** A group of shrubs and trees, usually evergreen but several are deciduous, which often bear needle-like or

narrow leaves. Usually they bear their seeds in cones.

**coppicing** The cutting back of shoots to near the base of a shrub or tree to encourage the development of young, pliable stems. Sometimes this is performed annually, but with some trees every three years – or more.

**cordon** A fruit tree (apple or pear) or a soft fruit (red or white currant) that is trained and pruned to form one, two, three or four stems. Mostly they are grown at a 45-degree angle, although some are upright.

**crown** The main branch system on a tree.

**dead-heading** The removal of dead flowers to prevent the development seeds.

**deciduous** A plant that each year sheds its leaves in autumn and develops a fresh set in the following spring.

**die back** The death of tips of shoots, the result of frost damage, faulty pruning techniques and, occasionally, after damage from pests and diseases.

**espalier** A tree – usually a fruiting type – with a vertical trunk and tiers of branches trained horizontally and secured to wires. Mostly, they are planted against a warm wall, but can also be trained up wires secured and strained between posts and not attached to a wall.

**evergreen** A plant which retains foliage throughout the year and therefore looks 'evergreen'. However, it is continually shedding leaves and developing others.

**eye** An immature growth bud. This term is especially applied to roses and also to grapevines.

**feathered** A maiden tree, with a few lateral shoots arising directly from the main stem. At this stage, it is at the beginning of its second year.

**fruit bud** Also known as a blossom bud, it is much fatter than a vegetative bud.

**girdling** The removal of bark in a complete circle from around a trunk. It is often confused with bark-ringing, when a narrow piece of bark

(from only part of the trunk) is removed to reduce vegetative growth. Girdling, however, is invariably performed with the intention of killing a tree.

**growing point** The extreme tip of roots or shoots.

**half-standard** A tree with a stem (trunk) 75cm–1.2m (2½–4ft) long between the ground and the lowest branch which forms the head.

**head** The part of a tree formed of branches, which are supported by the trunk.

**hybrid** A cross between two unrelated species. This can be between two species or, occasionally, two genera.

**lateral** A stem or shoot that arises directly from a main branch.

**leader** The leading shoot or main growth part of a branch. With a one-year-old tree this is the single shoot, while older trees will have several branches and on each of these there will be a leading shoot.

**maiden tree** A one-year-old tree, formed of a single stem with no shoots arising from it.

**nipping out** The removal of the tip of a shoot to encourage the development of sideshoots.

**node** The position on a stem where a leaf or shoot arises from it.

**pinching out** The removal of the tip of a shoot to encourage the development of sideshoots.

**pleaching** Training and pruning a line of trees planted close together to form a 'hedge' at their top. The base of each tree is free from branches, but at head-height and above their branches are interlaced. They are pruned to form a neat outline.

**pollard** Cutting back the main branches on a tree to near the top of the trunk. Pollarding is frequently performed to quickly and radically reduce a tree's size.

**pruning** The severing of parts of a tree or shrub to restrict or regulate growth, to shape or promote the development of flowers, stems and fruits.

**regulatory pruning** Pruning to remove weak, crowded and crossing shoots and branches.

**renewal pruning** Pruning to maintain a regular supply of young shoots.

**root-pruning** Severing roots on a tree to reduce its vigour and to encourage fruiting.

**rootstock** The part of a plant on which varieties are budded or grafted.

**scion** The varietal part of a plant and usually used to refer to the variety when budding and grafting. The rootstock is the other part.

**self-fertile** Varieties of fruit which are able to pollinate their own blossom.

**shrub** A woody plant with several shoots arising from ground level. Some plants can be grown as a tree or a shrub, depending on initial pruning and training.

**spur** A short, lateral branch which bears flower and fruit buds. Pruning encourages their development.

**standard** A tree with a stem (trunk) about 1.8m (6ft) long between the ground and the lowest branch which forms the head.

**stooling** Usually refers to a tree or shrub that is cut down to, or near, soil level to encourage the development of young shoots. These can be used when budding and grafting fruit trees. Alternatively, some ornamental shrubs (such as dogwoods) when annually cut down to near ground level produce attractive and colourful stems.

**stopping** The removal of the tip of a shoot to encourage the development of sideshoots.

**sub-lateral** A shoot which grows from a lateral shoot or branch.

**sucker** A shoot which grows from the stem or root of a grafted or budded plant, below the position where the varietal part and rootstock were united. On bush roses they grow from the roots, while on standard types from the stem.

**thinning** The removal of fruits or fruiting spurs so that the remaining ones have more light, air and space in which to develop.

**tree** A woody plant with a permanently clear stem between the ground and its branches.

**trunk** The woody structure between the roots and the branches.

**truss** A cluster of fruit or flowers.

**vegetative growth** Non-flowering, leafy growth.

**water shoots** Shoots which grow on the trunks of trees, often from where stems and branches were earlier removed.

**whip** A one-year-old (maiden) plant without any shoots.

**wound-paint** A special paint, usually with a fungicidal additive, used to coat pruning cuts to assist healing and to prevent disease.

# INDEX